Walking t
Summits
Somers
and Avon

CW00350586

Walking the Summits of Somerset and Avon

A newly charted route from Minehead to Chepstow

Hamish Brown

Patrick Stephens Limited

For Ray and Mary and shared miles between John O'Groats and Land's End.

First published in 1991

British Library Cataloguing in Publication Data
Brown, Hamish M. *1934–*
    Walking the summits of Somerset and Avon: a newly charted route from Minehead to Chepstow.
    1. Somerset – Visitors' guides   2. Avon – Visitors' guides
    I. Title
    914.23804859

    ISBN 1-85260-365-8

Patrick Stephens Limited is a member of the Haynes Publishing Group P.L.C., Sparkford, Nr Yeovil, Somerset BA22 7JJ.

Typeset by Burns & Smith Ltd, Derby

Printed in Great Britain by J. H. Haynes & Co. Ltd.

10 9 8 7 6 5 4 3 2 1

Contents

Whenever I hear men boast of hills, I will rise up in praise of the hills of North Somerset. The Devon hills are fair and woody, the Cornish hills are wild and craggy, but the hills of Somerset rise up to the sky clothed in the cloths of heaven.

H.V. Morton *In Search of England*

Acknowledgements

A book like this is dependent on many helpers. I must have visited, written to or telephoned every Tourist Office on the route, contacted every hostel, visited all the sites mentioned, looked at camp sites, pubs, B&Bs, museums and so on. Without exception I was given friendly help and advice which contributed much to my own enjoyment in exploring Somerset and Avon. The Somerset County Library, The Area Library in Street, The Central Library, Bristol and The National Library of Scotland gave help on many topics while my own local library (Kinghorn branch of the Kirkcaldy District Library) was unfailing in producing the dozens of titles requested over many months. Bodies like the National Trust, the Ramblers' Association and the various officers of planning and footpath departments of the local authorities all gave much help and, to test my text, many friends walked parts of it and reported back, others read the whole book, and several sources (individually acknowledged) provided that increasing rarity these days, the black and white photographs which I feel are such a vital part of showing the rich variety of the route. Lastly I cannot fail to thank Sheila Gallimore who typed my field notes and the staff of Kirkcaldy Instant Printing who photocopied everything at many stages. Thanks also to the following for their contributions: W.S. Barnard, Eddie Baxter Books, Basil Berry, Sue Blessitt, Norman Brade, The British Mountaineering Council, Graham Cheshire, Alice Clark, Ralph Clark, Jim Docherty, Doug and Jean Dyke, Andy Eddy,

Derek and Marian Emsley, Rosemary Evans, Bob Fells, Rick Hogben, John Holtham, Barbara Hooper, Geoff Jackman, Geoff Lloyd, Laurence Main, Chris Peart, Lesley Pettinger, Sylvia Popham, Bill Russell, Ray and Mary Swinburn, Nigel Vile, Deborah Walker/Plestor Photographics, the Curator and Committee for Aerial Photography, University of Cambridge, Bristol Cathedral Trust, City of Bristol Museum and Art Gallery, the SS *Great Britain* Maritime Heritage Centre, Cheddar Showcaves, and Wookey Hole Caves Ltd.

Introduction

When I walked from John o'Groats to Land's End one of the major interests was working out a satisfactory route linking these ends of mainland Britain. Almost naturally I found large sections of my route coincided with lengths of the West Highland Way, the Pennine Way and Offa's Dyke — not that I kept to them slavishly, but it was useful to have the available store of reading and information on these sections. For the bits in between I had to spend a great deal of time and effort on research, and even with this 'swotting' things often went wrong on the ground which meant an aggravating waste of time and effort.

During my Groats End Walk (and in the years since) I've been aware of many walkers with ambitions to walk the country end-to-end. Most lack the time to do it in one effort and many have pecked away, first at one set route and then another, to complete the South West Coastal Path, Offa's Dyke, Pennine Way, and West Highland Way. The missing links are usually left until last and often life's hectic business is too much, and the dream is crowded out by frantic reality. 'If only there were guide books to help' is the cry from the boots in the heart. Now at least a start has been made.

My route from Edale to Ruthin, largely using canal tow-paths, was practical and enjoyable and could be worked out easily enough from the book *Hamish's Groats End Walk* (Palladin). More recently I've seen a small guidebook called *A Cestrian Link Walk* by J. Davenport (Westmorland Gazette) which describes a route from Prestatyn to Edale, so that gap is filled. *A Borders to Highlands Walk* should follow shortly and I'm teasing away at the complicated far north in any spare time. In some ways the most complicated gap was the country between Minehead and Chepstow, the old Somerset of moors and gardens, cliffs and combes, cottages and castles, a part of Britain I fell for in the Indian summer that ended my Groats End Walk. The north east end of Somerset is now part of Avon, but for brevity I use Somerset in its older, complete sense.

The vision of a route through the length of Britain was a natural result of walking such a line. There are people who would scorn such a concept or say people doing this journey should be able to work out a route for themselves. Anyone who successfully does walk end to end certainly could, but the difficulty lies not in a lack of competence or confidence, as the critics suggest, but more in coping with the scale of one's personal practical problems. With the time-consuming research telescoped into a single book, people really can put feet to their dreams. The shouts of gratitude are, happily, louder than the moans of the self-appointed sneerers. No one is forcing them to buy a concept or a book so they have to call to criticize any other outdoor enthusiast for his particular inspiration. 'John o'Groats or bust' may be commendable. John o'Groats with some certainty is better. That certainty is based on the researches of others which makes practical guide books possible.

I'd often thought of this when stuck down some red, mud-oozing bridleway, with nettles up to the armpits and blackberry branches snarled in my hair, the rain belting down and a sudden realization that the hostel destination ahead was shut that day of the week. 'Oh for the simplicity of the Highlands!' I'd think, and then come out on a forgotten hamlet of thatched cottages and gardens of peacock colours, or top a rise to look on fabled Glastonbury arched by rainbows, or meet a friendly old shepherd (and his dog) who would dance the miles away with his cream-voiced yarns. The people of rural Somerset are the kindliest in England, the landscape and seascape an ever-changing delight, the walking superb. After the Groats End Walk I returned, not to fill in a missing link, but because here was some of the best walking in Britain. The summits of Somerset is a route worth walking for itself, even if there is no intention of linking long-distance paths end to end.

I realized that the Groats End Walk route through Somerset had the variety to make a good entity, but that line had missed out some of the best places so I determined to spend some time and work out a better way. The whole of one wet April was devoted to this, and one problem was frequently to the fore; mud. There is a large animal population in Somerset and their hooves can create conditions no sane walker would face, and time and again, rights of way on the map proved impossible in reality, their lines buried under growth that pointed to decades of neglect. By default we are losing thousands of miles of walking routes in England. A season of non-use could be almost as bad. When we gave a final test to the route and walked it in September places which had been straightforward in April gave us verdant battles reminiscent of tropical jungles (but the blackberries gave good eating!). Some of the bad bits of path on our route will, hopefully, be cleared by the authorities, but they are overworked and underfunded so can only tackle priorities. It gives them support if people write about places needing attention so please report on sections which are overgrown, horribly muddy or whatever. (Write to Rights of Way Section, Surveyors' Dept, County Hall, Taunton, Somerset TA1 4DY.)

This route was well tested in 1989 and if, in places, the description has to be field by field, this is preferable to going astray. In the Highlands it may suffice to say 'follow the stream for seven miles', for there may be no other features in that wet desert. The south–west of England has an altogether different appeal, a diversity which owes as much to man as to nature.

I found the crowds of tourists (in Dunster for example) quite astonishing, but the majority never go more than 400 yards from their cars. The joy of a walk like this is the complete freedom from the mechanical and social ties of most holidays. The call to cross the ridges and pass the rivers, to adventure onwards, is deep-rooted in man, however layered the urban gloss. That we have such freedom to roam in Britain is a joy, that we have such un-trodden ways of quiet walking in an area lapped by such vast flows of people I find astonishing. We last traversed the Quantocks on a September 'day of glory given' and only saw three other parties.

There has been no temptation to pad out this guide, rather a perpetual need to compress, so for places like Dunster or Glastonbury or Bristol I have given minimal additional information. There are good publications available in all these places which can be bought at the time. A guide is no more than a guide: the reader still has to do the planning and the walking. It would probably surprise insular Scots that walking in Somerset can be as strenuous as in Sutherland. Some days call for a briefer text as they offer mainly rural walking with little to break the rhythm, while some days need notes on a whole host of diversions. This variety is one of the walk's delights.

Some practical points. The route is described from Minehead to Chepstow as most of the other guides in existence take the same Land's End to John o'Groats direction. I'm not saying this is the best direction. (I first did it the other way round and found reading guide books backwards none too easy.)

Throughout it is assumed the reader is using the 1:50,000 map (nos. 181, 182 and 172 cover the route) and it is well to have the latest edition. I had to make extensive use of the 1:25,000 series but hopefully this text is adequate enough to leave them behind — there was a hefty pile of them! Only sketch maps are given as text and OS maps should be adequate. Heights are given in metres as that is what the map shows and to 'translate' becomes ever-more meaningless. However, most British walkers still seem to walk miles rather than kilometres, so distances are given in imperial units. Six-figure references are given when this is clearer than a long verbal description. Right and left banks of streams are always given as in the direction of flow, but to avoid any possible ambiguity I will say north bank, etc, rather than right or left.

At the heading of each day's walk the various map numbers are given. Bart means the Bartholomew 1:100,000, OSLR is the Ordnance Survey 1:50,000 Landranger and OSPF is the Ordnance Survey 1:25,000 Pathfinder. The day's mileage and metres of ascent are also given, with the cumulative total in brackets. These measurements are for the standard route described. You can do a quick estimate of feet of ascent by multiplying by 3 and adding a quarter of the original number.

Signposts abound in Somerset, and at crossroads or even on way-marking posts, when these point in our direction of travel the wording on the sign is given in brackets: 'Turn right past the first house (*Heathfield* ¾) ...' means that at the right turn there is a sign saying 'Heathfield ¾ mile'. Where there is more than one name indicated I only quote the vital one(s) and for the rest, abbreviate with etc, eg, (*Willet* ¼, etc) describes a signpost which says 'Willett ¼ Bishops Lydeard 5¾', but as the second place is irrelevant to our route, it is omitted.

I use the word 'path' for a way which is only practical for the pedestrian, though many are used by horses too. Paths regularly used by horses may be termed 'bridleways': a warning that the going is likely to be muddier than usual. The word 'track' covers a multitude of uses: forestry tracks, estate roads, old drove routes — but all could be motored over, although in some cases only by Land Rover type vehicles. By 'road' I imply a tarred surface which is usually open to public vehicle use.

Originally the route was very youth hostel orientated, but our first September visit rather forced us to rethink. We had reached Minehead in the morning and planned to walk to the hostel for the first night, but on being cautious and consulting the handbook I found the hostel was shut for most of September. Exford, our planned lodging the next night, coincided with the hostel's weekly closing night. When Crowcombe was also shut for weeks and at Street it was also a night off it became obvious that no route could rely on such unpredictability. Some of these hostels can still be used (and they are all hostels of character), but great care should be taken to check they are open and it is well to phone and book beds the night before. The information given is from the 1989 YH *Handbook* so is only a rough guide.

Camping is not so easy but where there are sites handy I've tried to mention them. On a walk of such regular ups and downs, packing a tent loses much of its attraction, but at least you can be off early. My biggest single objection to English B&Bs is the late breakfast (closely followed by the perpetual persecution of the standard breakfast fry-up). Keep asking for early breakfast though; water-dropping can wear away stony habit. In places where there is a great variety of accommodation I have not listed everything. Tourist offices can supply lists or, weekends and July and August excepted, you can risk turning up to look on the spot. In smaller places I've listed everything possible, but check these carefully because changes are frequent and booking ahead, even if only one night ahead, is advisable. Arriving wet, weary and late and *then* starting to look for a bed is apt to be discouraging! Two useful leaflets produced annually (send large SAE to Somerset Tourism, County Hall, Taunton, Somerset) are *Where to Stay* and *Caravan and Camping Sites.*

Many facilities, historical sites, and B&Bs have seasonal openings. Easter to the end of September sees most places open so double check outwith this period. April can be a delightful month and October's autumn colours make it a lure, but I don't like July and August. There are simply too many people and the climate can be airless and hot.

Busy roads have been avoided almost entirely because they are both dangerous and unpleasant for walking. Small rural lanes are used quite happily and sometimes in preference to cross-country opportunities where these are spoilt by difficult route-finding, obstacles or unfavourable conditions. Deviations are always made for good reasons, so don't be tempted by what look like short cuts. These have been tried and found wanting.

A score of Somerset friends walked a day, or days, or all of this route to see if my route descriptions were clear. In several cases further modifications had to be made because places became hopelessly overgrown in high summer. Tramping feet would help control this so some overgrown sections are still given as the route, or an alternative, but the need for a machete is clearly indicated! Perhaps some of the appropriate authorities might like to go and use their machetes, literally, *pro bono publico*. One Taunton lad who walked five days of the route wrote, 'Thanks indeed for providing some very interesting days of walking. I think we tend to forget what beautiful countryside we live in.' Lucky lad to have it on his doorstep.

This is not an official long-distance path with a multitude of facilities, so it is inadvisable to walk in large parties which would create problems (with accommodation for instance). Humans in a quiet landscape can create people-pollution. Tread quiet and treat soft. A party of two is probably the perfect size. Local B&B facilities may not cope with more than two people and solitary figures may be turned away by uncaring landladies. As far as I know all the route is on public footpaths or roads or open spaces like the summits of the hill ranges, so access should not be a problem, but much of the route is on sheep country and dogs are best left at home. I am devoted enough to my dog not to take him into such country. The landscape of our pleasure is the result of the local farmers' hard work over generations. In all the months of walking for this book I met nothing but kindness and helpfulness from local people, so treat them, and the landscape, kindly in return.

There is a 'Somerset Way' which runs from Minehead to Dunster, then heads south to Taunton and on east to Wells and Bath. This is less direct and misses the summits, but for those interested in Somerset rather than a Groats End Walk the 'Somerset Way' and this route could be combined. The only repetition would be Wells/Glastonbury and Dunster — and they always need more time anyway. See L. Main *A Somerset Way* (Thornhill Press).

The Summits of Somerset and Avon is laid out as an eleven-day trip but it could be shortened by two or three days (descending to Wheddon Cross direct, going direct from Wells to Bristol, or skipping a day in Bristol), *or* it could be extended to give another day in the Glastonbury-Wells-Cheddar area and dividing the last day into two so more time could be spent in Chepstow. Personally, I always want extra days.

There is so much to explore in Somerset and Avon. Descriptions and suggestions have to be kept to places and ideas on, or close to, the route; five miles off the route is planet-distance to the earth-bound plodder.

Sadly, one needs to plead with people to observe the country code of conduct. Please leave no litter. Don't climb fences, walls or hedges, cut through crops or let dogs run wild among livestock. Don't disturb wildlife. Avoid all fire risks. Close gates behind you. In other words, treat things as you'd like your own home to be treated. Say hello to those you meet on the way, whether locals or other visitors. And laugh when you go knee-deep in cow-green mud. You are walking for fun, remember!

Whilst every possible care has been taken to ensure the accuracy of this guide, the author does not accept any liability regarding the information or its interpretation by readers! Waymarkings can fade, signposts disappear, housing schemes obliterate paths and all manner of changes occur. Any guide goes out-of-date due to changes. Descriptions use obviously permanent features as much as possible but if you note changes — or any alteration or amendment you think would improve this guide — do please let me know. A reply is probably not possible but all such information will be filed and incorporated in any future edition. In choosing to walk such a route you choose to encounter its vagaries. I hope you enjoy this walk. I did.

Hamish M. Brown
Kinghorn

Day 1

Minehead and Dunster

Bart 3   OSLR 181   OSPF SS84/94
4 miles 40 metres

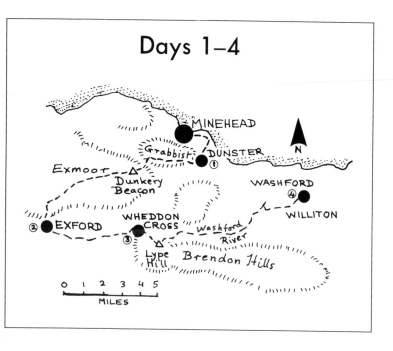

Travel to Minehead

The nearest BR mainline station is Taunton, 26 miles from Minehead. The Southern National bus line 218 connects the towns. Many other coach services run to Taunton or Minehead and there is also the unique West Somerset

Railway, Britain's longest private line, which operates both historic steam and diesel locomotives from Bishops Lydeard (bus connection with Taunton BR). Details from West Somerset Railway, The Station, Minehead, Somerset TA24 5BG, Tel: 0643 4996. For bus connections (Bristol/Bridgwater/Taunton/Exeter) contact Southern National, Tower Street Bus Station, Taunton, Somerset, Tel: 0823 272033.

Minehead

Minehead offers a wide range of services and accommodation besides all the touristy trappings. The only camp site is above the town (958470) in Higher Town, which also offers attractive B&B opportunities, but the steep pull-up — and in the wrong direction, so to speak —

Minehead Harbour, starting point for the walk. (Deborah Waller)

makes accommodation in the town itself more convenient. (One list I saw mentioned 50 hotels and B&Bs). There is a youth hostel a couple of miles inland, but perhaps the easiest option is to walk to Dunster and have the first night there.

Accommodation in Minehead is abundant. The Tourist Office, Market House, The Parade, Minehead, Somerset TA24 5NB, Tel: 0643 2624, can supply information for the Minehead-Dunster area and the West Somerset Booking and Information Office on the sea front near the station can do likewise, or make reservations. Tel: 0643 2396 (day) or 0643 5409 (evenings).

Minehead is a bustling holiday town but it has an open, friendly atmosphere and its sheltered setting in the lee of Exmoor is seen in the profusion of flowers and in the way café and pub tables spill out on to the Avenue. The old town round the harbour and up on the North Hill still retains a quieter atmosphere. For 500 years the old church on the hill has guided fishermen and traders into the harbour by a light at the rood loft window. Steps climb up the hill, reminding one of Clovelly, and Corsican pines clothe the slopes. There are grand views from St Michael's which, like most of the old churches we'll meet, is well worth exploring. I was rather taken by one tomb (*c.* 1410) for the dog at the figure's feet rests with his paws on a bone. There are no mines at Minehead, rather the name is probably from the old British *mynydd* meaning hill. Daniel Defoe noted the thriving port, but the herring and wool exports have long gone and so have many of the old fishmen's houses. A 'great fire' largely destroyed much of the Lower (Middle) Town in 1791. The *Waverley*, Britain's last paddle steamer in service, had deserted her home waters of the Clyde and was an odd sight in these waters.

Minehead to Dunster

The shortest route is $2\frac{1}{2}$ miles but is on tarred road, hilly and not altogether safe, while a walk along the sea is only a mile longer and very pleasant, so is the preferred route.

From the station turn east along The Strand (Warren Road) but do take a look back, for the height of North Hill rising above town and bay is attractive and, for those who have

Ready for the off in Minehead.

---

tramped the Coastal Path, evocative. We pass a brash array
of amusements and the vast sprawl of the Somerwest World
holiday complex, to reach the golf clubhouse at the end of
the road. A sign on the clubhouse wall indicates 'Footpath to
Dunster Beach' and pops one through to an altogether more
pleasant, quieter world of sea and sand and the waving green
of the golf links which bear the name of The Warren. To
those more used to northern climes there is a great variety of
seaside flowers. The changing shape of the land can be seen
in the submarine forest off Warren Point and, later, on
walking up to Dunster over the meadows, it is hard to
imagine this was once sea and Dunster a port.

Walk right to the end of the golf course and keep a wary
eye on the flying golf balls. (I trust a penalty stroke is the price
for hitting any walker.) Two well-preserved wartime pillboxes
stand near the end of the links and ahead is the large chalet
village of Dunster Beach. Do not go into this but turn inland
on a footpath alongside the stream just inside the trees. From
here to Dunster there are small *Public Footpath* signs and/or
direction arrows.

The path brings one to a charming old bridge. Turn left over this and follow the farm track to Old Manor (Guest House) which is a fifteenth-century building with a chapel built over the porch. The road is now tarred and runs on past Lower Marsh Farm (one September we noted a field of maize growing here) and over a level crossing. After a quarter of a mile there is a road junction. Turn left (*Dunster Beach* $\frac{3}{4}$) then, almost at once, go over a stile to follow a path up beside the stream. Note the old bridge which now leads nowhere or, rather, just across to the houses whose gardens dip colourful flowers into the stream. Below the keystone is a tablet inscribed 'Wm. and Geo. Rawle. Masons 1772'. The glasshouses on the map have been replaced by a housing development.

The footpath (signed *Dunster Castle*) follows the edge of a couple of fields beside the stream, and reaches a gate on to the A39 at Loxhole Bridge. On the way a footbridge across the stream should be ignored. Cross the A39 diagonally, right, to enter the castle parkland by a gate half hidden below the big chestnut trees. Technically we have now entered Exmoor National Park and only exit as we leave the Brendon Hills. A list of Park publications is available from Exmoor House, Dulverton, Somerset TA22 9HL (enclose an SAE). The grassy footpath crosses the drive to Dunster Castle (sign) and runs up to pass left of the car parks to a gate which leads one back to the busy tourist world — car part, toilets, Park Information Office, sheepskin factory shop etc. Welcome to Dunster.

The less pleasant road route to Dunster is as follows. From the station turn inland along Minehead's main street, The Avenue, and then take the second street left. This is Tregonwell Road which in turn becomes Ponsford Road and then Alcombe Road. When this joins the A39, Bircham Road, cross and turn up Church Street (church on the right) to reach the Britannia Inn. This village of Alcombe is now just an extension of Minehead rather than a separate place. There are shops and a variety of accommodation is available. If one turns right at the inn, on to Manor Road, this road leads on up to the misleadingly named Minehead Youth Hostel. The road becomes rough as it enters the combe and the hostel enjoys a peaceful setting under the wooded hills. If staying at the hostel it is possible to cut up directly on to Grabbist Hill but this would mean missing Dunster. Minehead Youth Hostel, Alcombe Combe, Minehead, Somerset TA24 6EW, Tel: 0643 2595. March and October, closed Sunday, Monday, 24 April–30 September, closed Sunday. Opens 5 pm. Evening meal 6.30 pm.

The left fork at the Britannia Inn, Combeland Road, runs straight to Dunster, rising to pass between Grabbist Hill and the bump of Conygar Hill, before dipping into Dunster. The tower on top of Conygar Hill is a folly; a similar tower was planned for the summit of Dunkery Beacon but, mercifully, never materialized. Just before the first houses of Dunster is the stump of the Butter Cross. (It used to mark the centre of the West Street market site but was moved here in 1825.) Carry on down into the town.

Dunster

Accommodation in Dunster should present no problem, since every other building seems to be a B&B or to be offering something for the tourist. A local in Skye once told me, 'Aye, we have two industries here, the sheep and the tourists — and we fleece the both of them.' In Dunster they don't have the sheep. The small town is really a very friendly community which has made it its business to look after visitors well. Cream teas, home-made ice-cream and a variety of evening meal possibilities will more than satisfy the inner man. If a frantic Spring Bank Holiday was not the best first meeting with Dunster, staying there soon revealed its real charms: old buildings and gardens, quaint corners and tidy houses. There is a castle on the dominant hill, occupied since 1070, a mill mentioned in *Domesday Book*, and still working, a medieval dovecot with 500 nests, an ancient church in a garden setting, an old packbridge which in the time of Henry VIII was given the name Gallox Bridge, a venerable tithe barn and the

---

Above right   *Thatched cottages in Dunster.*

Right   *Dunster Castle from the once seaward side.* (Deborah Waller)

The old dovecot in Dunster.

The Yarn Market, Dunster's most famous landmark. (Deborah Waller)

much-photographed Tudor Yarn Market. You need perhaps rather more time than is available to explore all that, but most people want to return to dainty Dunster.

The castle on its elevated hill dominates the town yet it is a friendly place with gardens and terraced walks and sited in a beautiful deer park, its scarred history mellowed by gracious living. *Domesday Book* mentions Dunster for the castle was given to the de Mohuns, followers of King William, who dispossessed the Saxons of their stronghold. The castle was besieged by King Stephen. In 1376 it was bought by the Luttrell family and was largely rebuilt in Elizabethan times. The Luttrells have been there ever since. Cromwell's forces, under Robert Blake, besieged it in 1645-6, forcing the Royalists to surrender after 160 days. A bedroom has a small closet where Charles II, when Prince of Wales, was hidden. Many of the fine furnishings date from the seventeenth century. Stancy Castle in Thomas Hardy's *A Laodician* is Dunster Castle and it is, of course, pictured in *Lorna Doone*. The castle was given to the National Trust in 1976. Open Sunday–Thursday, 11 am–5 pm, April to September.

The Luttrells dominate the town as much as does the castle. The unusual Yarn Market at the end of the High Street, where the farmers local cloth 'Dunster' was sold, was built by George Luttrell about 1609 and repaired after the Civil War. Facing the Yarn Market is the Luttrell Arms Hotel, which has an outstanding Jacobean interior. Originally built as a town house for the abbots of Cleeve, then purchased by the Luttrells in 1499, it became an inn, The Ship, appropriately enough, for Dunster was then a port of sorts (though the river has long since silted up).

The High Street becomes Church Street and on it is the misnamed Nunnery, a slate-hung building dating to the fourteenth Century when it was built as the guest house of Dunster Priory. The only other Priory building to survive is the dovecote and it is in poor shape. There is also an old tithe barn. The church is dedicated to St George and is famous (or infamous) for its bells which chime a different tune each day of the week and carols at Christmas! Its magnificent rood screen is the longest in England. Luttrell monuments abound as befits such tenacious tenure. Just along from the church is the secluded and peaceful village garden, which

Above *The old 'nunnery' in Dunster.*

Left *Dunster Church, the first of many superb Somerset churches on the walk.*

was once the castle's kitchen garden.

The most curious attraction in Dunster is a model village sited up the rockery bank of a garden next to the Castle Gate. This oddity is not at all twee as one might fear, so don't miss popping in to see it.

The unusual model village in the garden next to the Castle Gates, Dunster.

Day 2

Grabbist Hill, Dunkery Beacon

Bart 3   OSLR 181
OSPF SS84/94   SS83/93
12 miles (16) 675 metres (715)

The traverse of Grabbist Hill

Grabbist Hill is one of my favourite belvederes and its traverse must be one of the most pleasant parts of our route. The transformation from busy Dunster to quiet woods is sudden and complete. Looking down over Dunster before starting up through the woods I was told, 'I want to be buried 'ere so Ise can always be admiring the view.'

Dunster is really one long main street, wide as the High

Looking back to Dunster from the path up Grabbist Hill.

Street (with the Yarn market), wide as West Street (with its many B&Bs) and joined by the narrow, tortuous Church Street (controlled by traffic lights). Near the West Street traffic lights St George's Street leads off, beside a building which was once the Methodist Chapel. Go up St George's Street and turn off left just beyond the school (*Grabbist*). There is a fine thatched house beyond our lane and opposite is Priory Green where the old dovecot and tithe barn are sited.

Our route goes up past the school and a graveyard, then turns left along beside the town's allotment gardens, becoming a path up into the woods above another, modern graveyard. Once in the wood there is a signpost (*Wootton Courtenay* $3\frac{1}{2}$, *etc*) which points us left. There is also a yellow waymark and these will be with us to the trig point on top of the ridge. The whole of Grabbist Hill and beyond is a maze of paths and tracks of all sizes so the markers are quite useful. Just round the first corner take a right fork uphill. This is known as the Goosey Path. (Above is another route, the Duckey Path.) There are many young Spanish chestnut trees, hollies and sturdy oaks, and in spring there is a bedlam of birdsong to match the beautiful forest: one autumn we were followed by a noisy green woodpecker. Owls hooting may

The fine path along the crest of Grabbist Hill.

turn out to be the West Somerset Steam Railway!

Our path steepens and then you are suddenly on the crest of Grabbist Hill with a dramatic view down to Minehead and the Severn estuary. (If starting from the Youth Hostel go out of the back gate and turn left for 200 yards to pick up the red *Dunster* waymarkings up on to the crest.)

Somewhere along here the Victorian hymn-writer Mrs C.F. Alexander was so moved by the view that she sat and wrote the words of *All Things Bright and Beautiful*. The 'purple headed mountain' is Dunkery and 'the river running by' is the Avill. I've not found Blindman's Well which is marked on the 1:25,000 map.

Turning left along the crest we are soon on an open moor of gorse, heathers and young birch, with fantastic views. Across the Avill valley the circle of a ring fort stands out clearly on the dome of the first hill, Gallax Hill. Follow the obvious main track to the trees, then where the track enters the forest at a gate skirt right to follow along outside the forest, its edge an ancient dyke lost among the roots of a parade of beech trees. A little further on there are trees on the right, cutting off the sea view, but a clear ride leads on. The next landmark is the crossing of the main Timberscombe–Minehead bridleway, a spot I'll not forget as I once became entangled there with the local hunt, a noisy collection of horses and hounds. There is a four-armed signpost. We simply carry on along the crest, where the track is really two parallel paths, and the ground to the right is open again.

There are tracks criss-crossing everywhere as we draw near to the 295 trig point, but the vital junction for us is just before the trig on the old wall, rather hidden by trees. There is a seat and a Tilhill fire-warning sign. Grabbist Hill is really the spur above Dunster and this summit appears to have no name. (When there once I asked a local about a name and he nodded at the sign and said, 'Tilhill.') A spot height 297 lies

_____

Top right   *The view down to Minehead from Grabbist Hill.*

Middle right   *At the highest point on the path for Grabbist Hill.*

Right   *Looking back to Wootton Courtenay.*

200 yards off in the conifers so is strictly speaking the summit of the marvellous ridge.

The crossing just before the 295 trig is marked by another four-armed signpost. We now desert our yellow route for the red indication of *Wootton Courtenay 1*, but at the first junction take the right fork, a long straight track which is then joined by tracks coming in from the right, before tackling a steeper and steeper descent as a sunken lane, the old way from Minehead to Wootton Courtenay.

When the village is reached the Dunkery Beacon Hotel is immediately on the right, a well-placed refreshment stop. There is a village store (half days Tuesday, Saturday, Sunday) along the road to the left, and a working mill is now a pottery of note. The church has a fifteenth-century roof with some of the finest carved bosses in the west and there are some interesting features inside. A rector from there became the first Bishop of Colombo in what is now Sri Lanka. Flowery gardens make this village particularly attractive but with the journey's longest uphill waiting we had better push on. Dunkery beckons!

Under Dunkery Beacon — the thatched farm with the pheasant on the roof.

The traverse of Dunkery Beacon

Leave the hotel by the west exit (note the pet dog graves at the back of the lawn) where there is a triple junction in the road from the village. Take the left fork for *Brockwell ½, etc.* At Brockwell a thatched house has a pheasant finial on the roof. At the junction beyond there is a sign indicating *Dunkery Beacon 150 yards on right* but a short cut path (jungly in summer) leads from behind the sign up on to this path which wends through trees before gaining the heathery moor. The route is clearly signposted at any junctions or crossings. (The path can be seen clearly from the Inn at Wootton Courtenay.) The most surprising crossing is that of a motor road at 443 metres, just 1 mile off the summit of Exmoor. On the summit of the shoulder which we ascended are two big prehistoric cairns: Robin How and Joaney How.

A broad, firm track leads from the road up to Dunkery Beacon, 519 metres (1,704 feet), with its big cairn, view indicator and inevitable prohibitory notices. The cairn informs us that Dunkery was given to the National Trust in 1935, and

Walking up Dunkery Beacon, with Wootton Courtenay and Grabbist Hill beyond.

in fact the Trust owns all the summit ridge and most of the ground northwards to the Channel. There are remains of tumuli and a bare patch where beacon fires have been lit over the centuries. In 1897 the Jubilee crowds present were able to count 44 other beacons. Dunkery, not surprisingly, is a fantastic viewpoint.

The Bristol Channel dominates the view northwards, with Wales usually just discernible; southwards you may catch a glint of the English Channel and only the dark mass of Dartmoor (Yes Tor can be picked out) is higher as the eye circles the landscape. The TV booster mast on Lype Hill is the highest point for the morrow and, beyond the Quantocks, you may just make out the shadowy Mendip ridge.

Exmoor Forest, covering about 120 square miles, is mainly in Somerset, but the National Park also includes a bit of Devon and about 13,710 acres of National Trust property. A charter of the time of King John mentions it as a royal forest. Its history is an interesting story of man's fight to reclaim the bleak slopes. It is mostly slate and sandstone and the uncultivated moors are covered in tussock grass, heather and furze. Black grouse may be seen on these moors above Exford. Dunkery Beacon now has a 'letter-box' similar to those found on Dartmoor, with stamps for your record. It lies in a depression about 50 paces from the big cairn (140°).

Two main tracks head west from Dunkery Beacon, the first dips and rises on the crest to Rowbarrows, the second descends gently to run along above the sturdy old hedge marking the upper limits of cultivation of Codsend Moors. Rowbarrows (510 metres) is a collection of old cairns and the path veers off from there to the north-west so one has to angle down across the largely trackless heather to gain the track along the hedgerow. This leads to a road junction at 455 metres. *Exford 2¼* is indicated, but half a mile down the road there is a crossing, with *Porlock 6½*, right, and a red

Above right *Nearing the summit of Dunkery Beacon, with the Brendon Hills beyond.*

Right *Dunkery Beacon, the highest point in Somerset and the highest point on the walk.*

waymarked bridleway for Exford, left. This unsurfaced road left is taken and then we turn through a gate into the second field, go straight down this, passing to the left of a jutting corner of wall, to a gate in the corner. Beyond the gate the field edge is followed and thereafter sunken land takes us steeply into the valley of the River Exe. The descent is well waymarked or indicated.

Exford

The richness of the valley contrasts with the windy heights. One of the often unconscious delights of Exmoor is its freedom from massed afforestation, but while I would like to think this is for aesthetic reasons it is probably just too harsh a world for conifers. Exmoor Forest in centuries past was a Royal Forest for hunting, and had nothing to do with trees, and a few solitary trees were famous for being so unusual.

I've never had a wickedly wild day on Exmoor, to which the local reaction is always, 'Huh, you're lucky.' The quicker way off to Wheddon Cross might be advisable in nasty conditions but the moor, sun or storm, is a place to return to again and again. We may come over its highest point but we still only touch the edge of Exmoor. The great snow described in *Lorna Doone* is by no means uncommon. Alas, *Lorna Doone* country lies beyond our pedestrian reach.

My first visit to Dunkery Beacon, on my *Groats End Walk*, was a grim enough morning, but not wild. I wrote, 'The mist oozed about, and imagination crouched with John Ridd watching the Doones ride by — the opening scene of *Lorna Doone*. He was a lad then, riding home from school in Tiverton after his father had been killed and, here, by the light of the flaming beacon, he fearfully, secretly, watched the raiders pass.' I walked right across the crest of the moor then and down to Lynton, a memorable day.

The veracity of the Doone legends is a fruitful source of debate, but tradition has it that the murder of a child whose mother they abducted from Exford finally roused the countryside to storm their stronghold. Exford (another *Doomsday Book* place) is peaceable enough now, a straggly hamlet on the roads that criss-cross the River Exe at this point. The bridge is the scene of an escapade of the

A view across the Green in Exford.

highwayman, Tom Faggus, in *Lorna Doone*. The church is high on the road to Wheddon Cross, and its typical West Country fan-vaulted screen came from a church near Watchet, replacing one lost in over-zealous Victorian restorations. (The screen had been crated, in pieces, for decades before a church where it would fit was found. Exford raised £700 for it; now it would be regarded as priceless.) The Methodist Church has two Burne-Jones windows. The Devon and Somerset staghounds have their kennels here and fishing is also popular so Barbour jacket accents mix with those of the colourful tourists. It is hard to imagine this peaceful hamlet suffering any upheaval, but the rains that led to the Lynmouth disaster in 1952 caused water to pour over the green and flood the houses beyond. The first thing the village store knew was water spurting through the letterbox.

There are three hotels, several B&Bs, a youth hostel and camp sites in or near Exford. The Exford Stores and the Post Office both display local information on accommodation so this can be checked on arrival.

The Exmoor House Hotel, Exford, Minehead, Somerset TA24 7PY, Tel: 064383 304, is reasonably priced. The White Horse, Exford, Minehead, Somerset, Tel: 064383 229 offers good food but is more expensive and not everyone will enjoy the bar decor of foxes' brushes. The Crown Hotel Exford, Minehead, Somerset TA24 7PP, Tel: 064383 554/5 is more upmarket.

The youth hostel, Exe Mead, Exford, Minehead, Somerset TA24 7PU, Tel: 064383 288 is open 5 pm, 21 March–31 August. 1–30 September, closed Sunday. Evening meal 7 pm.

Sunnyside (B&B) is on the corner as one reaches the Porlock road entering Exford. Tel: 064383 586.

Court Farm is on the outskirts conveniently beside tomorrow's route. Court Farm, Exford, Minehead, Somerset TA24 7LY, Tel: 064383 207.

Edgcott House, recommended, is out on the Porlock road. Edgcott House, Exford, Minehead, Somerset, TA24 7QG, Tel: 064383 495. Open all year.

The nearest camp site, Downscombe Farm, Tel: 064383 239, lies one mile out on the Edgcott road, and further up the River Exe is Westermill Farm campsite (shop, showers, etc), Tel: 064383 238. Staying there would allow a longer walk along the moors, over Almsworthy Common to descend steeply by a small road.

Day 3

Exford to Wheddon Cross

Bart 3   OSLR 181   OSPF SS83/93
5 miles (21) 260 metres (975)

Hills and combes

The 6 miles to Wheddon Cross is a bit of a switchback but gives a sample of the rich Exmoor farmlands and a contrast to the heathery heights of yesterday. As the Exe cuts deeply down among the hills our route is a gentle one compared to any route further south. Leave Exford by a road opposite The Crown which passes the garage to a car park and picnic area (Paths to *Winsford 4½, etc*). Red markings indicate our route as far as the Staddonhill Road.

Follow the River Exe through two fields then turn left (*Winsford 4¼, etc*) up the farm track crossing from Court Farm, (accommodation, recommended). This leads through two fields to a gate and, beyond, walk left along the hedge to another gate. Cross the field ahead in the same line (through gaps in the hedge) and Higher Combe Farm will be seen ahead: the route drops down and then up to it with a footbridge over the stream.

Turn left at the farm road (*Winsford via Staddon Hill 3½*) and walk up the lane to a minor tarred road, Staddon Hill road. Turn **left** (the red markings point right), then at the T-junction turn right and follow the road down into Larcombe, but just before the road swings right at the foot, angle off through a gate on the left on to a farm track.

This fords a small stream and twists up to a long strip of field to the left of an old quarry. Cross the gate at the top of this field and follow the hedge of the field beyond to a gate

The converted mill near Luckwell Bridge.

leading into an old green lane. This leads up to the narrow but tarred Thorne Lane. Turn right.

This is great country for buzzards. Between Exford and here last time we saw seven, and had to laugh when one buzzard pulled up over a hedge on seeing us just as a magpie flew over from the other side. 'Near miss' is I think the aeronautical term. A very undignified near miss.

Walk down to Oldrey Cross, the junction with the road into Oldrey Farm. Opposite the farm road, between two field entrances, is a narrow bridleway between high hedges. Follow this as it loops down to the hamlet of Luckwell Bridge, a corruption of St Luke's Bridge. This bridleway is often very muddy and overgrown so the right-of-way going down the fields may be better. See OSPF 83/93. Before the bridge,

The Rest & Be Thankful, and the Sundial Stores, Wheddon Cross.

over the Quarme, yellow waymarkings and *Weddon Cross 1½* point right, a pleasant route on track and path which takes one past an old mill converted into a house, a pathside spring, old mine workings, a squat standing stone of white quartzite (right, in a field after going through a gate), a footbridge (where we disturbed another buzzard sitting on a tree) and finally a rather deep-cut bridleway ('steps' cut by pony feet) up to Wheddon Cross. When muddy this last inescapable bit can be toilsome. From the top the views back are rather fine. A gate leads into the cricket ground. Walk round the outfield, left, to reach the car park of The Rest & Be Thankful Inn.

Wheddon Cross is an open, fresh hamlet looking up to Dunkery Beacon, and backed by the patchwork of the

Brendon Hills is perhaps the highest village of Exmoor. As few visitors stop, other than for refreshments, this is a good overnight base. The Rest & Be Thankful Inn does excellent bar lunches. (The public loo in the car park is oddly signposted for 'Ladies' and 'Men.')

The Sundial shop and tea-room (closed Monday, Thursday, 064384 283) offers an extraordinary range of services besides a shop and home baking: hairdresser, birthday cakes to order, flowers and plants, portrait photography and an art gallery. The name comes from the Victorian sundial over the door, which since the building was then a watchmaker's could have been an ironic trade symbol. The dial's face is graduated from 5 am to 4 pm, for being on an east wall it goes into shadow long before summer sunset. I suspect the mastercraftsman who made it had a sense of humour. We are given the latitude of Wheddon Cross and told this is also the latitude of Ostend, Düsseldorf and Blagoveshchensk! The Latin motto *Tempus edax rerum* (time, devourer of all) is one we can ignore on this the shortest day of the walk.

The view across to Wheddon Cross.

Those who would like a more active day could follow the footpaths along the River Exe for 5 miles to Winsford which many regard as Exmoor's most beautiful village, have lunch there (in the thatched Royal Oak perhaps), explore the church which so dominates the village, count the bridges and then head off for Wheddon Cross — steeply up north-east (Furzehill Lane), north (Ison Lane) to Oldrey, where one joins the described route to Luckwell Bridge and Wheddon Cross. The A396 is too dangerous for pedestrians.

Wheddon Cross has two B&B accommodation choices opposite The Rest & Be Thankful: Exmoor House, Wheddon Cross, Minehead, Somerset TA24 7DU, Tel: 064384 432 and Dunkery View, Wheddon Cross, Minehead, Somerset, Tel: 064384 220. On the B3224 is Higherley, Wheddon Cross, Minehead, Somerset, Tel: 064384 582 and, down a lane off it, is the most attractive and welcoming farmhouse accommodation of Little Quarme, Wheddon Cross, Minehead, Somerset TA24 7EA, Tel: 064384 249. Also, more upmarket, Raleigh Manor House Hotel, Wheddon Cross, Minehead, Somerset, Tel: 064384 484.

Dunkery Beacon direct to Wheddon Cross

Wheddon Cross can be reached by descending directly off Dunkery Beacon. Follow the path from the Beacon to Dunkery Gate. From the south side of the bridge the route is well marked in red all the way to Wheddon Cross. Start down this right bank (*Wheddon Cross 2½*), cross the small field and turn into the wood. The path keeps along its upper edge to start with and then goes through grand oak woods which often ring with the yaffle of woodpeckers. If you are lucky you may even see red deer. You eventually come on to the road about 300 yards below Blagdon Cross. Turn left, steeply down, then, shortly after a lane comes in, turn right (*Wheddon Cross 1*) on a path which skirts Raleigh Manor House Hotel and by Watercombe Farm leads up to Wheddon Cross village.

The National Park has England's largest herd of red deer. The heart of Exmoor was once a royal hunting preserve but the deer now may well be found in the wooded combes, their natural environment. They may be more easily heard than seen in the autumn when the mating rut keeps the stags roaring — a sound sometimes described as what you might hear from a desperately sick cow! Deer calves should never be touched — the mother hind will be nearby. Like everything else in nature; look, like, and leave. Unique in a way deer are not are the Exmoor ponies whose origins are unknown and who still roam Exmoor. In winter they grow an insulating undercoat.

Day 4

Brendon Hills, Washford River

Bart 3   OSLR 181
OSPF SS83/93   ST04/14
13 miles (34) 145 metres (1,120)

Lype Hill

Forested or farmed, with deep combes running down to the sea, the Brendon Hills have a charm of their own. The road that runs along the crest, milestoned by barrows, with huge panoramic views, would make an interesting route but, sadly, the traffic on it has increased (and too many cars treat it as a racetrack), so after climbing up to Lype Hill, the highest point, we descend to follow the quieter, secretive River Washford as far as Cleeve Abbey before cutting over to Williton for the night. A harder day to make up for yesterday.

On the ascent of Lype Hill, with Dunkery Beacon beyond.

From Wheddon Cross go along past the post office, passing to the right of the war memorial (*Cutcombe only*) and then, almost at once, swing off right again for *Putham*, walking up a deep-cut, narrow road, Popery Lane. At the first minor crossroads, Cutcombe Cross, we turn right, picking up red markings (*Luxborough via Pitleigh 5½*) and ascending by a lane and then field edges to reach Pitleigh Farm. There are gates galore for the next few miles: please shut them behind you. The route nearing the farm is edged by a deep combe but the big hedges rather block the views north.

At Pitleigh take the lane between hedges, left of the white gates and right of the obvious house, to reach a field. The hedge is followed to a gate and thereafter the route goes alongside a fence, the posts clearly marked with red. Several fields later, one approaches the end of a line of beach trees on the skyline, and the route turns sharp left to go along by these trees. An enclosure juts out and beyond is a gate taking us eastwards again. From the gate aim for the gate in the **middle** of the hedge opposite, which lets us on to the minor road that runs down to Timberscombe. We cross the road to the gate on the other side to gain what was once Lype Common.

From the gate cut diagonally left across to the projecting corner of the field, not to the gate directly opposite, then make another diagonal to a gate in the fence ahead (red mark) and then aim to pass **north** of the enclosure with the trig point of Lype Hill, 423. Several tumuli are shown on the map and even the trig perches on one. The view all the way up widens steadily and Lype Hill is a fitting climax to the Brendons ascent. The TV booster mast rises from the trees not far off and our route over Exmoor is in full view — for the last time. The footpaths on maps and on the ground are confusing on Lype Common but the following is marked and clear.

Follow the fence past the trig eastwards to the next gate. The route bears left at about 45° (there is a red mark on a telegraph pole) to a gate — with a gun barrel view down Druid's Combe and the Washford River. Cross the next field in the same line and then walk along by the field edges (all well marked). There is a gate about 50 yards up from the line of stumps of the hedge bordering the old common. Go through the gate and down to this lopped hedge (yellow/red mark) and turn right along it to the corner of the field. There is a signpost indicating *Luxborough* (yellow mark) and *Luxborough via Chargot* (red mark). The former descends almost directly for Churchtown/Luxborough, which is soon clearly visible, and is the simpler choice. Luxborough is really a double entity, with its Churchtown up on the hill and its Pooltown down in the valley. Kingsbridge is the bridge itself, in Pooltown. The map's Pooltown is a farm.

The steep track puts in a couple of zigzags to reach the stream of the infant Washford. One can cross and pull up to Churchtown/Luxborough then drop steeply down the road to Kingsbridge but it is less of an effort to follow the valley bottom; there are a couple of field edges down to the small

Looking across to Luxborough. (Deborah Waller)

tarred road going over to Chargot and Pooltown. Walk up it for about 200 yards to take the first track breaking off left. Go along, passing right of a caravan, and follow the woodland path/track by the river. Nearing Kingsbridge cross a footbridge (one plank and a handrail) to follow down the other bank. One exits through some sheds and the welcoming pub, parts of which are 500 years old, lies across the road.

Washford River

Leave by the Washford road which is simply followed for six miles to that town, a varied route with another pub conveniently at the half way stage. The road is tarred but a quiet one and the river is a cheery companion. At the cost of a toil uphill one could fork left not long after leaving Kingsbridge to go up through Slowley Wood (appropriate

The welcome inn at the start of the walk down the Washford River. (W. Russell)

A quiet corner in the upper Washford River valley.

name!). There is a big view from the top where one turns off right to Felons Oak and on down to Washford.

There are some attractive houses as one leaves Kingsbridge and some fine dwellings will also be seen across the river. The walk down to Roadwater is mostly shaded by trees, very welcome on a hot day, the first miles being through Druid's Combe. Roadwater is a charming sprawl of village which is really joined on to Lower Roadwater. There is plenty of human interest: a craft workshop on entering, the Valiant Soldier pub which also does B&B, as does Orchard House, a village shop and an antique shop, Junk and Disorderly. Half a mile on, right, is a holy well.

An old mineral line once ran from Watchet along the Washford Valley to Roadwater and then turned off up a side combe to reach the mineworkings on top of the Brendon

Above *On the upper Washford River.* (Deborah Waller)

Top right *The gateway to Cleeve Abbey near Washford.*

Right *Inside Cleeve Abbey.*

Bottom right *The mosaic floor in front of the Abbey.*

Hills. The Incline (024343) is an unusual feature which can still be made out: a ramp, nearly a mile long at a uniform 1:4 gradient down which the wagons of iron ore travelled before going on to Watchet for shipping across to Ebbw Vale in South Wales. Roger Sellick in *The Old Mineral Line* (Exmoor Press) gives an interesting account of all the workings.

Follow the now open valley down to Hungerford (where the White Horse pub does farmhouse B&B) and Cleeve Abbey, a site not to be missed. We take a cross-country line from Hungerford/Torre to Williton (to avoid the lethal A39), but the abbey is near enough to visit and Washford's services may be welcomed.

Cleeve Abbey to Williton

Cleeve Abbey is satisfying at every level: the setting is beautiful, the surroundings are spotless and the buildings can interest layman as well as specialist. The Earl of Lincoln founded this Cistercian abbey in the twelfth century and

The beautiful roof in Cleeve Abbey — once used for storing hay!

though the church has almost vanished some other parts are well preserved. (Usually it is the other way round.) The fifteenth-century refectory with its massive wagon roof is the most impressive feature. Once ivy-clad and used as a byre it is now seen as having one of the great roofs from that period to have survived. A sweep of stairs leads to this hall. Some medieval floor tiles have survived too (right round the back), there is a big rose window and some beautiful vaulting that was so perfectly crafted that it has never been touched since. One enters the site through a gabled gatehouse with unusual features. (Cleeve is an English Heritage site: small fee, literature available.)

The Washford Inn is residential and does good food (Tel: 0984 40256). Next to it is the West Somerset Railway Museum. Campers may be advised to continue down to the coast where there are several sites, catching up on the morrow by Five Bells and Williton. But to return to Cleeve Abbey.

Walk back to Hungerford and keep on the Monksilver road past the White Horse. There is a row of cottages with pleasant gardens then the road swings left past the Coach House (a minor road goes off right). At the end of the first field turn left along a farm track to a cement works. A footpath heads off, right, at the entrance. Take this and continue along a field edge overhung by oaks to a gate in the top right corner. This leads to a sunken tunnel of a path which can be impassable in summer with head-high nettles! Some spectacularly big leaves of hart's tongue grow on its banks. We skirted through field edges for 50 yards of the worst of this path, but hopefully it is one that the authorities will tackle sooner rather than later. The path leads to the clutter of Bardon, an old house which (in 1988) was sadly neglected. The right of way does a northern circuit of the house and rejoins the drive at the gates.

Cross the B3190 and continue to a T-junction. Turn right. At the next junction turn left and just short of the A39 (you can see the signpost of the junction) turn right along a concrete farm road. Walk through the farm, keeping right of an arched corrugated-iron shed, and exit by a gate in the wall. You are looking down on a building which gave me one of the walk's moments of serendipity. Orchard Mill is a combination of mill museum, garden, craft shop and restaurant, a very welcome stop. (Evening meals to order. Closed Monday in summer, Monday and Tuesday in spring, autumn; Tel: 0984 32133.) The mill was originally built in 1616 and milling continued until 1967. Restored in 1979 it is now a comprehensive museum with over a thousand items of country life.

The drive from the mill joins the road past St Peter's church (a 1666 alabaster font its best item) and a left turn at the school leads to the A39. Turn right and the centre of Williton lies to hand. There are at least six hotels and several B&Bs so accommodation should be no problem. Many are on Long

The museum and restaurant at Orchard Mill, by Williton. (Deborah Waller)

Street, the A39 heading out for Bridgwater. (The name dates to 1472.) On the same street is the hospital (which was once a large workhouse!) and a station for the West Somerset Railway. Turning along the A358 Taunton road offers one attractive option, Blackmores, 6 High Street, Williton, Somerset TA4 4NW, Tel: 0984 32227. This is a new/ secondhand bookshop and tea room and also serves good evening meals and B&B. Further on is Beans and Things, a vegetarian and wholefood restaurant. If one turns off onto Half Acre (opposite the Wyndham Arms), then first right, on the next corner is the Williton Pottery. Sited in the old village forge this is a working pottery, using West Country clay to produce an exceptional range of attractive wares in traditional Somerset style. There is an excellent display, and it is well worth a visit. Open until 6 pm.

Williton is a busy but unpretentious town, sometimes crowded with A39 traffic, but quiet in the evenings. Old sites have largely disappeared. The Wyndham family, to the fore politically in the eighteenth century, has been based on Orchard Wyndham since the early sixteenth century. Williton's main 'name' is Sir Reginald Fitz Urse — one of Becket's murderers! He had to sell half his manor here to go on a penitential journey to Rome and Jerusalem. Life was pretty tough not so long ago, too: in 1801 nine men were hanged in Williton for stealing bread.

A Somerset speciality you may discover at Williton is skittles, played indoors with enthusiasm, in hostelries throughout the area. So if there are mysterious rumblings intruding on sleep, don't worry; the hotel is not haunted, it is just they're playing skittles in the basement. A good sleep is recommended. The morrow offers what several people consider the most demanding day's walk of the trip.

The pottery in Williton. (Deborah Waller)

Crossing the Quantocks

Bart 7   OSLR 181 and 182
OSPF ST04/14, ST03/13 and ST23/33
20 miles (54) 540 metres (1,660)

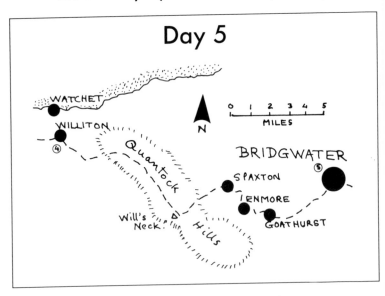

The Quantock crest

The earliest written mention of the Quantocks is in a charter of King Centwine of the West Saxons in 682, granting Glastonbury various 'parcels of land'. The higher ground of the Quantocks made it into a 'highway' from earliest times, so we are very late on the scene.

Take the road opposite the Wyndham Arms on the High

Street. This is Half Acre, which becomes Catwell and the tarmac ends at a private car park. When I passed once there was a notice (on the left as one continues on the unsurfaced track) begging, 'Mr and Mrs Dog. Keep off Grass Please.' There is also a mounting block. The track swings right to an old iron kissing gate — a tight fit for rucksacks — then a path sets off along the wall to edge a couple of fields to a gate where a farm track is picked up and followed on through Sampford Mill Farm (088406) to reach the A358 at a petrol filling station. After the first field, train buffs may like to cut over to visit a footbridge leading to a crossing of the railway line. There are Great Western Railway signs threatening 40/- fines if gates are left open! Study the timetable beforehand and you might coincide with a steam loco.

Cross the A358 into the village of Sampford Brett. Keep left past the church and when the road swings right keep ahead, beside a house, to a gate with a sign for *Woolston* and *Vellow*. Walk up the stream bank then cross a footbridge and along the field to a stile into a lane. Turn right at the minor road and follow it through the hamlet of Woolston, cross the railway and, after a telephone box, reach the dangerous A358 again. From the telephone box cross the A358 to the road heading for the hills: *Weacombe 1, etc.* Go up this for just over half a mile and as the road swings left there is a track off right, beside a pavilion-like gatehouse. *Weacombe Hill* and *Bicknoller Post* $1\frac{1}{3}$ *m* are welcome hill walkers' directives. After 30 yards the track forks. Take the gate between to pass round the shingled house and on uphill to a T-junction. Turn right, then a wide grassy track swings left, ascending parallel with Bicknoller Combe. Bracken has been taking over from heather on these slopes for many years now. Weacombe Combe (a bit of tautology) separates us from Beacon Hill and The Great Road, once the historic track to Holford. Bicknoller Post is said to mark the site of a change house. Quantock ponies must have been sturdy beasts. This is a sweeping view out to sea. We ascend to the top of Bicknoller Combe, a narrow neck with the fingers of Hodder's Combe running down to Holford on the other side. Paths and tracks radiate in all directions and there are tumuli in plenty. We are now up on what Wordsworth described as 'smooth Quantock's airy ridges'.

Bicknoller Post on Weacombe Hill. (Deborah Waller)

The most useful track curves up to skirt east of Thorncombe Hill, rises, then dips to the Halsway Post (141385), another criss-crossing of paths and another cross-ridge pass. Halsway Soggs is the splendid name for the moister upper reaches of Halsway Combe, while the underlying rock of this end of the Quantocks bears the friendly name of Hangman grits. The track climbs up to pass east of Hurley Beacon. Left there is a scatter of tumuli to the 358 trig point of Black Hill. The track angles down to the trees rimming the woody combe above Crowcombe (more magpies than crows) to reach Crowcombe Park Gate, but it is worthwhile diverting to Black Hill which many hold to be the best view from the Quantock crest. Crowcombe Park Gate is just that: a gate into the park. There is even a gatehouse lodge. Continuing along the upper tree level the track soon comes to Crowcombe Coombe Gate where one finds the only motor road to cross the Quantocks in the central, highest part of the ridgeway. Crowcombe Coombe Gate is

The Brendon Hills from the Quantocks.

On top of the Quantock Hills, at Black Hill trig point.

not given on the Landranger map, but it lies just above the upper set of double chevrons which indicate the steep descent to Crowcombe.

Continue SE along the line of beeches. Sometimes there are two rows with a sunken lane between. You can walk along outside the trees equally easily. People must have used this Hare Path as it is called for thousands of years, and the walking really is delightful. After 1½ miles the Triscombe Stone is reached, a small, stumpy monolith regarded by the superstitious as a wishing stone. On a misty day with the trees creaking and buzzards mewing in the clouds it can be quite atmospheric. A motor road comes up from the north-east by Cockercombe but doesn't cross the crest. The other side is bitten into by Triscombe Quarry. Ahead the ridge swells up to Will's Neck and the track swings on up to its summit, a dark swelling among the greens. Richard Jeffries noticed this effect too, writing of 'massive Will's Neck, which stands out in black shadow defined and distinct, like a fragment of night in the bright light of day'.

On the Quantocks.

On the pull up to Will's Neck.

Will's Neck, the highest point on the Quantock Hills.

Will's Neck trig point 384 metres (1,260 feet), the top of the Quantocks, is a sweep of dark heather-brown set above the bright greens on either hand: a uniquely rich English scene. My first visit here was on a chill Good Friday morning but as I reached the summit the first skylark of the year rose, ringing into a blue window in the clouds. The Somerset Levels stretch inland from Bridgwater Bay — so on a clear day the line of the next few day's walking can be observed. We will not be as high again. Dunkery Beacon and Minehead can be seen as well, a grand view. The Quantock's scenic value was given official recognition in 1957 when it became the first ever Area of Outstanding Natural Beauty. Even with the swamp of conifers on the north-east flank there is a rich variety of wildlife, including plenty of deer. The tree variety makes for the bird variety: the nuthatch, which works down tree trunks and eats nuts etc, and the tree creeper, which works up tree trunks and eats insects, are two birds you may be lucky to see. The goldcrest, our tiniest bird, also works in the conifer canopy.

To descend from Will's Neck take a path north-east, leading directly to the edge of the major plantations. You descend a track outside the forest, looking down on Aisholt Common, a pleasant open route. Nearing the foot you join the road out from Aisholt hamlet. Aisholt lies across the valley which Coleridge called 'a deep, romantic chasm'. He wanted to live there but his wife thought it too remote and they opted for Nether Stowey instead. (Sir Henry Newbolt did stay at Aisholt in the 1930s). Coleridge wrote *The Ancient Mariner* here (and Watchet is regarded as the setting) and was interrupted by 'a person from Porlock' when writing out the dream poem *Kubla Khan.* The Wordsworths also stayed in Somerset, T.S. Eliot is buried in East Coker, Arthur C. Clarke was Somerset born and bred, Fay Weldon has set many of her stories in the area, and Evelyn Waugh ended his days in Somerset.

Cross-country to Bridgwater

Continue downwards, swinging right (*Taunton/Bridgwater* signs at junctions) to drop steeply (and on to OSLR 182) to reach Hawkridge Reservoir. Follow the road along by the reservoir, built in the early 1960s to supply water to

Hawkridge Reservoir. (Deborah Waller)

Bridgwater. A yacht club, fisherman and coots play on its waters. (There is a car park, toilet area just off the road.) In under a mile the hamlet of Spaxton is reached, though the town sign is sited a long way out. The Victoria Inn is on the left and just beyond we then turn right for the wiggly road to Pightley. The Spaxton church interior has some superb woodwork: pews, bench ends, pulpit, etc, but as it is a bit off route perhaps only the real enthusiast will take it in. Between Spaxton and Enmore lies the site of a weird sect, the Agapemone, which existed here for many years. A curate from nearby Charlynch, H.J. Prince, 'The Beloved' gathered together a number of well-to-do ladies in the last century, who lived well, if secretively. Despite claims of immortality, the founder died in 1899, and was succeeded by a priest who had charge of the London Agapemonite church and who, after proclaiming himself the new Messiah, had to flee London. He came to Spaxton with his wife and a young woman, the 'Spiritual Bride of the Lamb', who bore him three children: Glory, Power and Hallelujah. The Messiah died in 1927 and in 1962 the property was sold.

The map shows plenty of the red dotted lines indicating rights of way, but alas these are (almost invariably) 'lost', the parks ploughed up and turned into fields, or neglect seeing them rank with blackberries and nettles. This is very disappointing. Only where farmers use them regularly are the tracks sure and clear — but then they may be ankle deep in mud. The easy answer is simply to keep to the quietest roads. At least there is not much traffic and, with sunken lanes and blind corners, cars can't travel too fast. I spent two unrewarding days teasing away at likely paths so, believe me, what follows is the best of a bad job. My companion on one walk called it a road fit for a demented grand old Duke of York. There are some ups and downs.

At Pightley turn left round Pightley Corner, which sounds

Barford House. (Deborah Waller)

like something out of *Winnie the Pooh*. The next feature is Barford House which is sometimes open to the public and can be seen from the white entrance gates where our road swings right. The house was long empty but has been restored: a fine brick mansion, with a walled garden and rich parkland. Enmore's 'castle' can be seen across the valley but the map indicated paths have gone. Twice over the wellies in cow sludge convinced me there was no option to the haul up and down again to reach Enmore, but maybe Barford-Enmore paths can be improved. Maize fields were something unusual to northern eyes, and the trees bowed down under tons of apples. This is rich landscape by any standard.

We pull up to a T-junction, turning left down into Enmore. This road is an old pack route up onto the Quantock crest at Park End. If we have had to toil up, the reward is an expanded view. The first building in Enmore is the school. The kids were at their games in the yard when we passed, for all the world like Breughel's painting. Only the clothes have changed. This was the first free primary school in England, set up in 1810.

The best of Enmore lies on the circular road by the church. The splendid church tower is fifteenth century, and there is a magnificent Jacobean oak pulpit and other relics inside. Enmore Castle is set amongst fine trees, a moated eighteenth century creation. William the Conqueror gave Enmore manor to the Malet family who held it for 22 generations until 1681 when it passed to the Earl of Egmont. A later earl built an extraordinary folly of a castle, with moat, drawbridge, etc. Most of this was destroyed in 1833 when the present house was built.

If you can find them open the Tynte Arms or the post office can provide refreshments.

The lane up past the post office and round behind Tirelands Farm to Cobb's Cross Farm is a fine old bridleway which proved impossibly overgrown one September, yet I walked it one April quite easily. (The nettles had not grown then!) A *Public Footpath* sign at the end, after an hour of bush-whacking, was not appreciated. Next time I'll keep to the zigzags of the road from Enmore to Goathurst, which is what I'd recommend from June onwards. Hopefully the state of this nice path will improve with use as feet trample the

Above left *Goathurst.*

Left *A cottage in Goathurst.*

Above *The seventeenth-century Halswell tomb in Goathurst Church.* (Deborah Waller)

---

shooting growth. (Another walker gave up the nettle-bashing when she nearly stood on a snake!)

Goathurst is almost a parody of 'ye olde worlde' village. I'm sure it's made of sugar. Bags of apples were appreciated for which there was a can for payment, contributions going to the local church fund. We munched Gloucesters and let our feet cool down. (There is a small post office/store.) The first house on entering was called Witts End and half way along was Toad Hall. The church is another old one, with assorted memorials to the Tyntes family, whose Tudor house, Halswell, dominates the village, the park famous for its red deer and a heronry. There is a strangely carved pillar in the churchyard. The Tynte family pew has a 'squint' cut through the wall to the altar. The real gem is Sir Nicholas

Halswell's 1633 tomb: a canopied mausoleum with effigies of the knight and his wife flanked by nine 'weepers', his six sons and three daughters.

At the east end of Goathurst where the road turns right, go up past the telephone box and take the gate into the field to follow along the hedge. Just **before** the hedge turns left there is a gate. This is the route, and **not** straight ahead up to trees on a rise. Walk down the edge of this field and through a gate, turn right, then the track swaps to the other side of the hedge line and runs along the edge of several fields to the farm of Oakenford. Being the only access to various fields this right of way should stay clear! Oakenford has a dairy farm's rich ground patina but the drive is solid concrete.

Turn right on to the road then left at the next junction to pass the big farm of Rhode. The outskirts of Bridgwater are reached after $1\frac{1}{4}$ miles and another half a mile leads to the arterial A38. Turn left for the town centre, unless seeking White Horse in the Black Horse. Bridgwater is a busy market town with a population of over 30,000, but it is often missed by the tourist — which is to our gain.

Bridgwater

When we turn left onto the A38, Taunton Road, there is an initial group of B&Bs then, further on, it seems to be all B&Bs.

Round the central Church of St Mary and across the River Parrett on St John Street (in the direction of our tomorrow's walking) there are several other hotels and B&Bs. Some of the commercial hotels are reasonable and there are also some very up-market hotels. The campsite shown between the A38 and M5 south of the town no long exists, but there is a rather remote site at Greenway Farm (274374) on Skimmerton Lane, Wembdon, Tel: 0278 457262.

The Tourist Office is at the Town Hall on High Street, Tel: 0278 427652. Next door is Rhyme and Reason, a good bookshop for maps etc. High Street lies just north of St Mary's Church and the Blake statue now looks down a pedestrianized Fore Street. On my original visit I wrote that the admiral seemed to be taking a step back in horror at the traffic congestion, although now the town centre is much more relaxed for visitors. Not having a car is a great simplification.

There is a Blake Museum too, in Blake Street, a continuation of George Street which runs off Fore Street (open all year, 11 am–5 pm, Sunday 2–5 pm. Tel: 0278 456127. Admission free). This successful commander of Cromwell's Commonwealth forces was born here in 1598 and there are documents and displays about him. Blake rose to fame through his dour defence of Taunton and went on to become the most inspiring sea captain of pre-Nelson times. He cleared the seas of the rival Dutch, smoked the Barbary pirates from their lairs and humbled the Spaniards. Relics and a video about the Battle of Sedgemoor and the Bloody Assizes may help clarify a nasty period of history for us. Sedgemoor is on our route tomorrow.

Bridgwater is old without appearing ancient: much has been rebuilt and rebuilt and, while hardly beautiful, it is a lively place as befits the administrative centre and market town for Sedgemoor. There are two annual events of note: at

The Blake statue in Bridgwater, with the tall spire of St Mary's in the background.

the end of September St Matthew's Fair, dating back to 1379, is one of the largest in England with streets filled with stallholders and acres of fairground attractions, besides the serious agricultural elements; in November (the Thursday closest to 5 November) there is the Carnival, when 80 huge floats wend through the town in a riot of colour and sound. (November Carnivals also take place at Glastonbury and Wells).

On my *Groats End Walk* my evening stroll in the suburbs was given a jolt when I found a Chinese dragon prancing along the road — no doubt practising for the Carnival. I'd been hoping to see the tidal bore run up the River Parrett. The quays, docks and warehouses have been transformed into a marina and tourist attraction, and the town centre has been partly pedestrianized. The town's main feature is the slender-spired church of St Mary's, which has stood there since the fifteenth century and provides a useful landmark for the centre of the town. The spire itself is 179 feet high and dates from 1367, which I always find rather marvellous. The interior of the church has been altered considerably but has interesting monuments, a Jacobean screen and a fifteenth-century pulpit. The big seventeenth-century Deposition painting was originally captured at sea from the Spaniards and auctioned off at Plymouth. The medieval castle (where Monmouth was 'crowned'), the hospital, the friary, have all gone. Castle Street and others show attractive eighteenth-century styles so most of the centre of the town is a conservation area.

Day 6

The Somerset Levels

Bart 7   OSLR 182
OSPF ST23/33   ST43/53
13 miles (67) 90 metres (1,750)

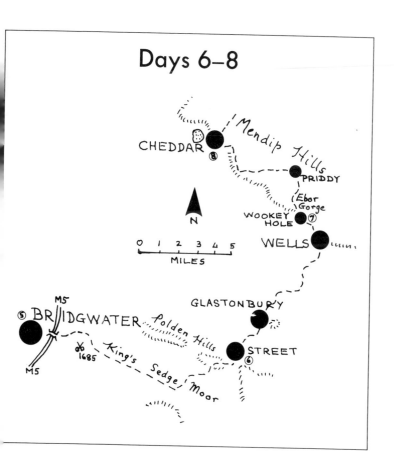

Days 6–8

CHEDDAR ⑧

Mendip Hills

PRIDDY

Ebor Gorge

WOOKEY HOLE ⑦

N

0 1 2 3 4 5
MILES

WELLS

GLASTONBURY

M5
⑤ BRIDGWATER   Polden Hills

✠ 1685   King's Sedge Moor

M5

STREET ⑥

On the Levels to Street

The way out from Bridgwater is surprisingly quiet while the walk through the Somerset Levels will be a unique experience. Walton Hill (only 269 feet) with its view back, and its revelation of Glastonbury Tor is a fitting climax to a very unhilly day. There is plenty of history, however.

Since Admiral Blake stands pointing out the route, we'll walk out from there. Go down the pedestrian precinct of Cornhill to cross the River Parrett, still tidal to beyond Bridgwater. The clay and sand brought down by the Parrett has long been made into 'Bath brick' (named after the maker not the city). This bridge dates to 1883. We turn right along Salmon Parade to busy Broadway. Cross this on to curving Cranleigh Gardens, lined with a row of chestnut trees, to reach St John Street and the station. Turn off to the station and cross the railway by the footbridge, to the right of the station, which leads on to Redgate Street. Walk along this and, just before the factory building, turn left on to the fenced footpath which will take us to the suburb of Sydenham.

The footpath runs past some allotments and a football pitch to come out at the back of a row of houses. Bear left, then right opposite the garages, to debouch on to Longstone Avenue. Turn left, then first right on to Fairfax Road which leads to the dual carriageway of Parkway. Turn right, then go over at the pedestrian crossing to enter the playing fields. A path leads across the playing fields in rolling, drunken, Chestertonian fashion, passing left of a housing scheme. It continues down a rough lane, through a field and over a footbridge into another field (being built upon in 1989). Cross the new road and continue in a straight line until the path takes a twist half right to come on to Avebury Drive (beside number 14 — street names are not always immediately visible). At the end of the drive cross the bigger Eastern Avenue to gain a play area and another arm of houses, turning right down this (Palm Tree Close) between numbers 6 and 7. Turn left at the junction, then turn right at the end on to a path past a children's play frame to reach a country road (Bower Lane) which is only a field away from the M5. The noise of the motorway is an audio-guide. Cross the road (slightly left) into a field which leads to the pedestrian bridge

The 'other world' — looking down on the motorway leaving Bridgwater.

over the motorway. If the Devil took Jesus up to a high mountain to tempt him perhaps a modern replay could use his perch. It is the highest point for miles around and a grand viewpoint. (You may also, if the wind is south-westerly, catch a whiff of Bridgwater's instantly recognizable scent; M5 drivers can often tell where they are from the smell.)

Fleeing the Devil, cross the footbridge, turn left, through a gate (horse trough), then turn right to follow the hedge past a pylon to a stile 50 yards left of the corner of the field. Cross the next field to a footbridge over a ditch and join the farm track which leads into a big farm, Fisher's Farm (334370), from which a minor road leads along into the ancient hamlet of Chedzoy. Between Chedzoy and Westonzoyland the 1685 Battle of Sedgemoor took place, the last real battle on English soil. Victory may have gone to the king, but James II was to flee just three years later in the Glorious Revolution. The Duke of Monmouth was a bastard son of Charles II, a spoiled favourite and a bit of a chancer who landed, ill-prepared, to usurp the throne of his uncle. He gathered a force of virtually

unarmed peasants and rashly went into battle on Sedgemoor. The battle was a brave fiasco, which was the end of the 'Pitchfork Rebellion'. Monmouth fled but was captured, taken to London and beheaded on Tower Hill nine days after the inglorious battle. Judge Jeffreys' shameful 'Bloody Assize' saw 150 locals executed and over 800 transported to slavery in Barbados. Parts of *Lorna Doone* tell of Jan Ridd's near escape from becoming involved in the 'Pitchfork Rebellion' and Conan Doyle's *Micah Clarke* describes the battle. In 1688 the country had had enough of the king's Catholic imperialism and called on William of Orange.

Left *The extreme flatness of the Somerset Levels is well illustrated in this aerial view.* (Cambridge University Collection of Air Photographs; copyright reserved)

Below *The equestrian monument in Chedzoy Churchyard.* (Deborah Waller)

The road does a wiggle to pass the Church — one to stop and visit. The crest above the door is dated 1579, the pulpit dates to Edward VI and the font was originally Norman. The chancel roof is highly ornate, and the pew ends are all individually carved in this church of oak. Outside a buttress is worn where men sharpened scythe and axe blades before marching off to battle in 1685. Many of them were brought back and buried in the churchyard, unmarked unlike the knight inside whose effigy lies with a greyhound at its feet, or the fine equestrian bronze marking twentieth-century warfare.

The fabric fund of Chedzoy gains from a curious custom dating back to the fifteenth century. Every 21 years a piece of land is sold by auction, the auction continuing for the time it takes for half an inch of candle to burn out. The last bid before the flame died was the successful one. This auction last took place in the 1980s so it will be next century before you can witness it again!

The extreme flatness gives Pendon Hill and the rest of the Polden Hills along to Street an exaggerated height. Once past Parchey, rather than following the road to Sutton Mallet turn right on to the south bank of the King's Sedgemoor Drain which will become one of the journey's most vivid impressions, being the major water course of the district. It dates back to the 1790s. On a sunny spring day the larks will be singing overhead, while various ducks, 'unmute' swans, herons, redshanks and even cormorants splash on the waters of the drain: a remarkable experience which places the M5 in perspective. Just walk along the water channel for six miles which must be the briefest instruction in this book. There are a few stiles to cross on the way!

Those with a special interest in the Battle of Sedgemoor, or in churches, can cut over to visit Westonzoyland. With the battle being fought so near the church was highly involved. King's men and rebels alike were buried there, 22 of the latter first being hanged — the rebels tumbled into a common grave, the poor covering of which had the local people complaining a week later. Some 500 prisoners were locked in the church, and many of them were to die later. The rising was followed up by punishments which were to be seen again in 1745 after Culloden, the death of all Jacobite hopes

Top *Swans on the King's Sedgemoor Drain.*

Above *The incredible flatness of the King's Sedgemoor Drain landscape.*

The church is one of the finest in Somerset.

The *zoy* names, Chedzoy, Westonzoyland, Middlezoy, go back to Saxon times and have *island* elements in them, as does Othery (*other island*). The monks at Glastonbury encouraged large-scale reclamations round these island or

Above left *Somerset Levels.* (Deborah Waller)

Left *Westonzoyland Church.* (Deborah Waller)

Above *The historic interior of Westonzoyland Church.* (Deborah Waller)

---

semi-island sites, which were prosperous enough for each to have a notable parish church. Their towers milestone our walk along the King's Sedgemoor Drain.

Ways across this major drain are few and far between. There is one footbridge (372354) and, at Greylake Bridge, a sluice, as well as the busy A361. We abandon the King's Sedgemoor Drain at Cradle Bridge and walk north to Nythe, then turn right over a hump of bridge on to the two-mile straight road of Butleigh Moor. The levels and moors perhaps need explaining: the moors are not the usual grouse-noisy heathery uplands but flat, peat-based acres.

The country between the Quantocks and the Mendips was covered by sea almost into historic times. When the sea

Control gates at Greylake Bridge on the Somerset Levels.

retreated man soon made his way into the marshes and some of the wooden trackways laid down then have recently been dug out of the peat (several sites/museums at Meare). The great religious houses and other landlords began to claim land from the marshes, erecting banks and walls, straightening the rivers and digging channels (drains, rhynes — pronounced reens — and ditches in descending order of size), a process that only saw real success last century when pumping machinery could finally cope with the waters.

Just how flat the area is we can see today. After passing the M5 we do not cross a contour line until Walton Hill. Sadly the intensive grazing needs of today are affecting the wildlife of the Levels, a subject of some concern and controversy. The grazing may be the richest in the land but there are side effects which upset nature's fragile balance. One example led to an amusing mishap when I was exploring some years ago. A small drain was so completely overgrown with pestilential floating weed that my dog simply did not recognize there *was* any water — so he tried to walk across.

Turn left at the end of Butleigh Moor. Walton Hill and its wingless windmill is straight ahead, our next objective. Our

The old windmill on Walton Hill.

road comes to the one running along under Walton Hill. Across it (slightly right) is the entrance to a bridleway but, alas, I found it so overgrown as to be impassible after the first 30 yards.

Plans are afoot to clear it so have a look. You might be able to gain the stile on to the National Trust land at the property's south-west corner. A stile has been erected for a footpath up the edge of the field just outside and parallel to the overgrown bridleway. This leads up to the road along the crest of Walton Hill, a rather dangerous one for pedestrians so one is glad to cross another stile, almost at once, on to the National Trust land and so wander up the grassy slopes past the windmill building. It is a private house now, converted from the late nineteenth-century mill, which was on the site of a mill first mentioned in 1342. Walton Hill and Ivythorn Hill are National Trust lands so one can walk anywhere along the crest. There is a car park and, at the highest point 82 metres (269 feet) a viewing indicator. The view is out of all proportion to the height of the hill. As a sunset spot it can be marvellous and there is also the sudden first sighting of Glastonbury Tor to stir the imagination. Caught by a hail

Looking down on to the Somerset Levels from Walton Hill.

Street Youth Hostel.

storm on Walton Hill, I first viewed the tor floodlit against a black sky and arched over with a double rainbow.

Continue eastwards to a stile, rather hidden by scrub, at the end of the field and take the woodland path beyond. Wild clematis can smother the trees in summer and the area is a haunt of squirrels, badgers, foxes, wild birds (I always seem to spot green woodpeckers) and flowers. The path eventually pops out on to the road, which you should cross. The National Trust have laid out a path with trees and hedging to create a safe route along to the Ivythorn grounds. Where a steep road comes up from the south there is a stile/footpath on our path side which leads down field edges into Street. Our path enters a bit of older woodland then runs along grasslands to the youth hostel. Much of Ivythorn Hill is hazel which is again being coppiced and managed.

The hostel is an unlikely Swiss chalet, a small, friendly night stop in a splendid situation. It was built in 1914 for charitable Quaker uses and became the first hostel in the south-west in 1931. Street Youth Hostel, The Chalet, Ivythorn Hill, Street, Somerset BA16 OTZ, Tel: 0458 42961. April to September, closed Tuesdays, otherwise open 5 pm, evening meal 7 pm.

Not far beyond the hostel the road meets the B3151, on the other side of which is Marshall's Elm Farm which does B&B (which Thomas Hardy once enjoyed here) and has a campsite, Tel: 0458 42878. One of the earliest clashes of the Civil War occurred here and about 25 of King Charles's cavaliers were killed.

There are footpaths which can be followed off Ivythorn Hill into Street which saves having to walk down the rather dangerous B3151. One was mentioned before reaching the hostel and the hostel has a drive dropping north which can be used by those staying there. Just 200 yards east of the hostel, at the end of a grassy enclave in the trees, there is a stile and footpath also leading down. Both routes come out on a small road (Higher Brooks). Turn right (very briefly if the footpath was used) and find a footpath sign (*Middle Brooks 1*) which leads down over two fields into some houses. A quick right and a left leads out of Gooselade on to a bigger road, Middle Brooks. Turn right and follow the road to a junction, where turning left leads one down into Street.

Street is rather 'posh' and its hotels, all on the High Street, are a bit up-market (Bear Hotel Tel: 0458 42021; Mullions Hotel Tel: 0458 45110; Wessex Hotel Tel: 0458 43383), so it might be as easy to walk on to Glastonbury where there is a wider range of accommodation.

There is so much to see in Street—Glastonbury—Wells—Wookey Hole that one really should take an extra day for exploration. The minimal day would be to walk from Street to Wookey Hole with brief looks at Glastonbury Abbey, Wells Cathedral and the Wookey Hole caves. This route is described as Day Seven, however long you take.

Some people might prefer to visit the Shoe Museum in Street, then walk determinedly through to Wells for the rest of the day/overnight, then see Glastonbury the next day before walking on from Wells to Wookey Hole. Buses regularly link these towns and Cheddar, so you can always add extra sites/sights/days.

Day 7

Town and City

Bart 7   OSLR 182
OSPF ST43/53   ST44/54
10 miles (77) 260 metres (2,010)

Street to Glastonbury

Street dates back to the Dark Ages but all we see today is
fairly modern. C. & J. Clark *is* Street; they quadrupled its

Henry Moore sculpture in Street. (Deborah Waller)

population last century. The Clark brothers made sheepskin rugs and, with the smaller skins, slippers. Slippers and shoes came to dominate — and have done so ever since. The Clarks were a Quaker family. They influenced the whole social structure locally and this is reflected in the town's buildings which have a unity, a sort of 'garden city' atmosphere, a century before that concept found expression. The Shoe Museum, 40 High Street, is open Easter–October, Monday to Saturday, 10 am–4.30 pm, and is both unusual and fascinating. Admission is free.

Leaving Street simply follow the A39/Glastonbury signs. The River Brue is crossed at Pomparles (or Pons Perilis) Bridge and at once we are in the land of legends. Excalibur, the great sword of King Arthur, may have been hurled into the mere which existed here at that period. Take the first road right (Roman Way). Not long after it bears right and begins to climb uphill there is a flight of steps on the left. Take these up into the fields and follow the path along the crest of Wearyall (or Wyrrel) Hill which is another of the surprising viewpoints of our walk. Perhaps the happiest view of Glastonbury Tor is obtained from its modest summit. A surprise may be the amount of industrialism to the west. (The rest is moor on moor to remind of Glastonbury's original island setting.) The Romans grew vines on the south slopes of Wearyall Hill.

Soon after starting to descend, the path passes a 'Glastonbury thorn'. This was the site of the original thorn which, according to the legend, grew from the staff of Joseph of Arimathea when the saint stuck it in the ground after landing on Christmas Day AD30. Thought to be a Syrian species, *Craetegus monogyna* var. *praecox*, the thorn flowers at Christmas time as well as in the spring, so it is not surprising that legends grew up about it. The original was cut down by the Puritans but it had been propagated elsewhere so thorns still thrive at Glastonbury.

When the path reaches a stile cross into the road (another less satisfying path cuts down the field to the A39) and turn

Above right   *Glastonbury Tor across the Moors.*

Right   *Glastonbury Tor from Wearyall Hill.*

left along Hill Head. At the next crossroads left leads into the
town centre, straight on leads to the Rural Life Museum, the
Chalice Well and Glastonbury Tor. At this stage of the walk
often despair. There is too much to see in the time available
Glastonbury is too good to hurry so spend all morning
exploring it and walk to Well's for supper time. It doesn'
really matter if you miss something. You are bound to come
back!

Glastonbury

Glastonbury Abbey is one of the most renowned sites in the
British Isles. It is said to have been founded by Joseph o
Arimathea and to be the burial place of King Arthur. S
Patrick, St David and St Columba are all said to have beer
associated with Glastonbury, and even Christ was supposed
to have paid a visit. The first great church was burnt in 1184
Building continued almost to the Reformation when the las
Abbot, Richard Whiting, was hanged on the Tor, and the
Abbey closed in 1539.

Myth and legend give way to the early chartering of a
monastery in Glastonbury by King Ine in 688. Its rise to
importance is connected with St Dunstan (born locally ir
943) who introduced the Benedictine rule and founded its
school, under King Edgar's sponsorship, before moving to
become Archbishop of Canterbury. Kings Edmund, Edgar
and Edmund Ironside were buried in the Abbey. The origina
wattle church, a great asset as a pilgrim lure, and everything
else, was destroyed by a fire in 1184.

Rebuilding started at once and a boost was given to
funding by the 'discovery' in 1191 of a grave, identified by a
lead cross inscribed 'Here lies the famous King Arthur in the
Isle of Avalon', an inscription as fantastic as the 'history' o
Geoffrey of Monmouth which it echoes. Edward I visited
Glastonbury in 1278 and the bones were reburied before the
High Altar. PR is nothing new. *The Glastonbury Guide* puts i
nicely. 'Historians nowadays base their interpretation or
facts; this has the result of making their writings more truthfu
but perhaps less colourful.' Glastonbury does not lack ir
colour.

The dissolution under Henry VIII began the ruination of the

The Abbot's Kitchen, Glastonbury.

great church, its stones being sold off or pillaged for local house and road-building (the road to Wells for instance), so there is relatively little remaining. The town suffered but slowly grew into a market town for the area. In the nineteenth century a canal linked it with the Parrett estuary then came the Somerset and Dorset Railway — the 'Slow and Dirty' (or 'Slow and Jerky') — which finally fell victim to closure in 1966.

St Mary's Chapel, completed only two years after the great fire and the Abbot's Kitchen (early fourteenth century) are the most notable buildings but the whole site is beautiful and well-described. Glastonbury rightly retains its popularity.

The Abbey, with its 36 acres of parkland, is owned by the Church of England. Open all year, except Christmas Day, Tel: 0458 32267. The entrance faces Magdalene Street in the town centre and the Gatehouse has a shop. There is a museum and a continuous programme of improving facilities.

The Chalice Well (or Blood Spring) at the foot of the Tor has an ancient history of healing and symbolic associations with early Christian and Arthurian legends. The Chalice from the Last Supper was supposedly placed in its waters, after which the spring ran red. The water is rich in iron and flows at a constant 52°F 25,000 gallons a day. The well and its garden setting are run by a charitable trust and open all year with a small fee.

Glastonbury Tor is topped by St Michael's tower, though the church itself has gone and an earlier building was destroyed by an earthquake in 1275. There is an ever-growing literature on an ever-growing mythology to do with the Tor. Here, according to some, was Arthur's Avalon, here a great centre of Druidical influence, here a great Zodiac pattern, here a strong ley line. There are too many pitfalls for me to comment safely. The Tor itself is ringed by terraces — an amazing endeavour — which some view as a maze and others as cultivation areas. Archaeologists have found signs

Above left   *Glastonbury Abbey.*

Left   *Glastonbury Tor.*

The George & Pilgrims Hotel, Glastonbury.

of Norman and Saxon churches, a medieval priest's house, a Saxon cross and evidence of an Arthurian period hill fort. The Tor is in the care of the National Trust and is freely open at all times.

The Somerset Rural Life Museum at Abbey Farm on the corner of Bere Lane and Chilkwell Street is a splendid showpiece, and besides the permanent displays there is an ever-changing succession of exhibitions, events and craft demonstrations. There is a tea room, picnic area and shop — very much a place where a morning can slip by unnoticed. The fine Abbey Tithe Barn is fourteenth century. Open, weekdays 10 am–5 pm weekends 2–6 pm, Tel: 0458 32903.

The town itself is very pleasant and highly geared for the modern pilgrim/tourist. Tourist office is in Northload Street, Tel: 0458 32954. In the High Street the George & Pilgrims goes back to the time of Edward III. It was rebuilt between 1455–75, and ever since has been offering its services to those coming to Glastonbury. Few old buildings in the country can equal it. Tel: 0458 31146. Next to the hotel is the Tribunal, a medieval courthouse with a Tudor front and containing a museum covering, among other things, life in a lake village, with articles actually excavated on the Moors. A plaque in an alley at the White Hart commemorates the hanging of some of Monmouth's men. I'm always amazed so much has survived with such a bloody background.

There are still several fine churches, even if the Abbey has gone. St John's Church has one of the finest towers in Somerset, rebuilt in perpendicular style in the fifteenth century, and it has a wide range of treasures inside dating from that period. There is a Glastonbury thorn in the churchyard, and each Christmas sprigs are sent to the Queen. St Benedict's church was originally dedicated to the

A *Glastonbury thorn growing in the Abbey grounds.*

Irish saint Benignus who died at Meare in 470. Built by Abbo<
Bere *c.* 1500 this is another in perpendicular style.

There are several bookshops in Glastonbury: Gothic Image
in the High Street has books on all aspects of Glastonbury
(and related topics), Haddan's Bookshop, in Benedict Street
stocks older books.

Accommodation varies from homely B&Bs to the historic
George & Pilgrims. Askwell Farm, at Edgarley (515382) does
B&B as well as being a camp site. Glastonbury Tor rises
behind the site, the stuff of romance. There is at least one
other B&B on the way out to it, one off Lambrook Street and
several at the town end of Wells Road, the route out on the
next day. Two other camp sites are Isle of Avalon, Godney
Road (494397) Tel: 0458 33618 and The Old Oaks, Wick
(519395), Tel: 0458 31437.

On to Wells

Leave Glastonbury by the A39 *Wells Road.* There's a mile to
walk to escape suburbia. The humpy bridge goes over an
abandoned railway line, then Hartlake Bridge takes us over
on to Queen's Sedge Moor. Take the first turning right
(*Launcherley*) on to a long straight road, the Long Drove
Rhyne. Walk along it for $1\frac{1}{3}$ miles then turn left. The junction
is just before a line of pylons crosses the rhyne. The road
bends slightly to the right (with the Short Drove Rhyne
running off left) then pulls over a minor green hill of Somerset
to edge Pill Moor. A side road heads west to Coxley which
with North Wootton to the east of the Queen's Sedge Moor
has a vineyard, a modern revival of a harvest popular in
Roman times.

When our road makes another bend to the right we can cut
a corner off the wending road. From the gate at the bend aim
diagonally across to the centre of the hedge opposite where
there is a gap in the hedge's irregularity, invisible from the
gate. (The 1:25,000 is useful.) Walk up by the hedge and
turn right along the line of the telegraph posts which lead to a
gate back on to the road. At the next T-junction we can cut
the next meandering road section as well. On the north side
at the junction is a red iron gate, and from here aim for the
prominent white house in the distance (leftish). Pass a barn

(on your left) to reach a gate in the top left corner of the field. Walk on in line with the big Mendips TV mast (on Pen Hill) to reach a bridge on the River Sheppey; exit left of the house.

This is Woodford Bridge. Across it take the second gate on the right. From this iron gate aim for the top of the field, the apex being right of the rightmost of several solitary trees on the skyline. Go through a gate and just ahead turn right along the fence from another gate (yellow arrow markings). This big field is followed by two small ones (marks/stiles). Wells Cathedral is now clearly in view. When you reach the top corner of this last field turn right, down beside the hedge for 150 yards to a gate. The right of way (on all maps) now goes running off along the top of the field beyond the gate to pass under a power line and through a gate at the right edge of the Park Wood (the name applies to two separate areas of trees). Forty yards before the end of the field turn through a gate to follow the other side of the hedge on a track which crosses an old railway line and curves through the wood beyond. You

The gateway to the Bishop's Palace, Wells.

leave the wood to skirt up a couple of fields with the Cathedral and Bishop's Palace ahead, a view which can hardly have changed in centuries and makes this a real pilgrims' entrance to the city of Wells.

After walking along beside the moat, (the swans are reputed to pull a bell rope when hungry), turn left through a gatehouse (the Bishop's Eye) on to the Market Square. The Tourist Office is in the Town Hall, left, and the Cathedral is right through another gateway, the Penniless Porch. Wells may be our smallest city but its cathedral is one of the most magnificent and time can go very easily exploring hereabouts. As I said earlier, don't hurry it. If the day has largely gone, take another for Wells in the morning and Cheddar caves (by bus) in the afternoon. Wookey Hole and the Mendips to Cheddar will fill the next day and on to Bristol is a good day's tramp.

Wells has about 80 listed places offering accommodation, from simple B&Bs to historic inns. Information/list from the Tourist Office in the Town Hall, Market Place, Wells, Somerset, Tel; 0749 72552.

Wells has no really convenient camp site but there are two sites up at Wookey Hole and, nearer, at Haybridge Farm (533459). One tempting option is to take a bus from Wells to the entrance to Cheddar where there are two sites and camp there, returning next day to continue the walk — with the option of a day without the backpack, quite a treat. There are frequent buses. The A371 should not be walked under any circumstances. It is narrow and twisting with no pavement and often steep flanks of growth — deadly for a pedestrian. Wells bus station is off Priory Road (becomes the Glastonbury Road), Tel: 0749 73084. Taxis, Tel: 0749 78039/76114/22365.

Wells

Arthur Mee in his well-known book called Wells 'a matchless place'. It is unique, as an entity, and in its parts constantly leaves one gasping with astonishment. I've amused myself by sitting inside the cathedral just to watch the faces of visitors as they enter — and suddenly see the improbable, amazing, brilliant inverted arches. They look so utterly futuristic, never mind modern, yet incredibly they were built over 600 years ago (1338) when the watery soil of Wells was threatening to topple the tower. There had been a church here for 600 years before that. Wells is old as well as glorious.

King Ina (long before King Alfred) founded a shrine, the Normans followed the Saxons, but the building we admire today was completed in the twelfth and thirteenth centuries. Wells was never a monastic foundation so the cathedral and the houses of its clergy survived unscathed at the Reformation, when Glastonbury was soon reduced to the ruin we know today.

The West Front was hidden behind scaffolding for a decade and when it came down a few years ago there was a revelation of tiered, wedding-cake cleanness and beauty which few buildings anywhere match. The front is 150 feet

The beautiful West Front of Wells Cathedral.

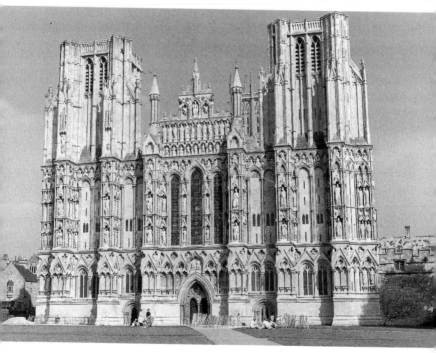

wide with tier on tier of figures (300 of them): lay, ecclesiastic, apostolic and angelic with a new statue of Christ over all. It is beyond praise. I watched a young man stand gazing upwards; he shook his head in wondrous disbelief and tears trickled down his cheeks. Not many buildings do that to us.

There are two solid towers flanking the West Front and, over the nave with its inverted arches, is the great tower, a strong edifice disguised with great grace. Leading down from the Chapter House is what has been called 'the most handsome stairway in England'. Then there is the Chain Bridge leading to the lovely Vicar's Close, the oldest

The astonishing reversed arches in Wells Cathedral. (Deborah Waller)

complete street in Europe; there are fine cloisters through which the Bishops of Bath and Wells have walked for centuries to the moated palace where they still live; there is the greatest assemblage of medieval sculpture in these islands; there is a famous show of stained glass; there is the unique astronomical/mechanical clock of 1390 which, on the quarter, has a strange figure who kicks his feet and strikes the hour while mounted knights charge round in a tournament. On the outside wall two knights in armour (jacks) strike bells with their battle axes.

These are just some of the major features. The setting is unequalled and the place buzzes with people. There is an

'Toothache' and 'thorn in foot' carvings in Wells Cathedral. (Deborah Waller)

excellent tea room/restaurant and shop in the cloisters
Masons are at work. There will be a service as like as not. It i
a living church which happily combines great and venerabl
antiquity with life at the end of the twentieth century. Wells i
my favourite cathedral in all England. Possibly this happ
atmosphere is old too; the original craftsmen so obviousl
loved their work. Just look at the misericords: there's a ma
riding backwards on a horse, an ape with a basket of fruit, *

The exterior of the medieval clock at Wells Cathedral.

mermaid and a lion, dragons biting each other's tails and a fox preaching to four geese, one of them asleep. Elsewhere there are stone carvings of a man suffering the agonies of toothache, a farmer chasing a fox which has stolen a goose, a man taking a thorn out of his foot, and a series shows fruit thieves getting chased, caught and beaten. One of the many monuments is to Bishop Kidder and his wife who were killed in bed when the Palace chimneys fell in a great November storm in 1703. This swept away the Eddystone lighthouse and sank hundreds of ships, including about a third of the English navy. The cathedral is open every day of the year. There is no charge but it would be a soulless person who will not put a donation in the offertory box.

The Bishop's Palace ('the most memorable of all Bishop's Palaces in England' according to Pevsner) has somewhat irregular hours but is open every day in August, office hours on Wednesday and Friday (May–September) and Thursday and Sunday afternoons (Easter–October), Tel: 0749 78691. The grand gateway over the moat leads to extensive grounds and buildings. St Andrew's Well still flows (its waters run down the main street!) and originally gave the town its name. The grounds have mature specimens of interesting trees: deodar, tree of Heaven, ginko, tulip tree, black walnut, etc. In times past Bath and Wells in turn became the seat of the Bishopric but, diplomatically, the title is now combined. Wells likes to think of itself as the smallest city in England. People are quite huffy if you call Wells a town.

The market place (market on Wednesday and Saturday) is surrounded by old coaching inns. From the windows of the Tudor Crown William Penn, founder of Pennsylvania, preached to vast crowds before being arrested. The drawbridge of the Palace was last raised in 1831 when rioting followed the Reform Act and the Bishop's Palace in Bristol was destroyed. The City Arms was the city gaol for 300 years. The Swan dates to 1422. The White Hart and the Star are also old coaching inns. There is a museum in the former Chancellor's House overlooking the Cathedral Green. Open daily, Monday–Friday, April–September; afternoons rest of the year; Sunday afternoon in summer. Wookey Hole's prehistoric collections are on display.

Somerset's largest parish church, St Cuthberts', has

impressive perpendicular architecture with a soaring 1430 pinnacled tower and would be better known were it not for the cathedral attracting all the visitors. (Some visitors are so impressed by its tower they assume this is the cathedral!) There are several medieval almshouses. A *Town Trail* leaflet is a good investment if really 'doing Wells'. A recent monument has the Olympic symbol on a pavement with a marked distance of 22 feet 2¼ inches, the distance Wells-born Mary Rand jumped for a gold medal in the 1964 Tokyo Games.

Wells hosts a Somerset School's Folk Dance Festival each June when, after a procession, performances by 2,000 children take place on the Cathedral Green. November sees the Winter Carnival, always the Friday nearest to 5 November.

In Tucker Street is Falkland House (Tel: 0749 77902), which has nothing (directly) to do with the royal town in Fife, but is an agency for selling the products of the Falkland Islands: fleeces, wool, crafts, philately items, books, etc. There was a spinning demonstration on when I first saw the place. I have to grab the chance of seeing films and one evening, after walking from Street, I happily watched *E.T.* in the Regal Cinema. A morning can disappear browsing in the secondhand bookshop, Courtyard Books, Old Palace Yard (off Priory Road, Tel: 0749 77112) or, for new books, in the West Side Book Shop in Sadler Street (Tel: 0749 76208).

To Wookey Hole

Leave Wells Market Place by going through the Penniless Porch and along the West Front of the Cathedral then turn right. Walk through the archway and turn left up Vicar's Close from the end of which steps lead up on to a street with the resounding name of The Liberty. Turn left, then right on to New Street at the mini-roundabout. Cross to the pillar box near where there is a small cobbled alleyway with a plaque indicating the start of the West Mendip Way (which, as we note it often, is abbreviated to WMW). One of its marker posts points us on for *Wookey Hole 2*. The West Mendip Way runs from Uphill, near Weston-super-Mare to Wells and was created to mark the Queen's Silver Jubilee. It now continues as the 'Mendip 40' to Shepton Mallet and on to Frome as the 'Wyvern Way' and 1990 should see it extended to Warminster and the Ridgeway.

About 70 yards along this lane turn right, then immediately left into Lovers' Walk, which runs alongside extensive playing fields. Turn right at a junction (WMW) and on up through school buildings to a kissing gate, edge a field and cross two roads (Ash Lane and Orchard Lea (WMW), up through the last of suburbia. Here the route merges with a rough track to join a corner of tarred road which is followed up to and along the fenced-off Underwood Quarry. At one time there was quite a protest over plans to enlarge this quarry at the expense of the right of way. In 1895 the citizens of Wells turned out in force, with pitchforks and scythes to march along this right-of-way and clear it of barriers which had been erected by the landowner. The town band led the army!

Walk round the edge of the quarry turning left at a memorial to Ella Gould, a retired schoolteacher and keen rambler who died in Nepal while trekking. (The WMW diverts.) After a gate there is the quarry of Milton Hill biting into the hill on the right. The limekilns (often overgrown) were in use until after the last war. The quarry is often used for practising abseiling and other climbing/caving techniques. The WMW crosses a kissing gate and in the top corner of the field beyond goes shooting off up Arthur's Point, a rather pointless diversion. Keep on along the track instead and turn right at the next *Wookey Hole* sign into a field, to follow along its edge to the spur coming down from the hill above, Arthur's Point. (Arthur is supposed to have spied out the land from here before descending to destroy the Witch of Wookey.) Passing a trough go through a gate (the WMW rejoins us) and follow two field edges to a kissing gate on to the road at the start of the buildings of Wookey Hole. Walk along Coombe Brook, the main road, passing Homestead Park, a luxurious camp site, left, . (Tel: 0749 73022), the post office (tea room and shop as well, left) and just before Wookey Hole Inn (accommodation, right) turn down a short alley to cross a bridge and so gain the Wookey Hole Caves complex: vast car parks, toilets, café and restaurant, obviously a popular attraction, and for all the hype the 'Wonders of Wookey Hole' should not be missed. Do remove the mud from your boots before going into the buildings. Several houses in the area do B&B and Ebborlands Farm (527477) has a camp site (Tel: 0749 72550).

The Mendips are riddled with caves large and small, natural and developed, offering a whole range of activity. Here, as at Cheddar, there is an emphasis on touristy visiting but less obvious there is also serious exploration to challenge some of the country's best cave experts. The River Axe has carved out a variety of caverns and shafts and walkways carry the visitor along this underground river world with its intriguing features — including the Witch of Wookey. A stalagmite in the first chamber resembles a witch's profile but generations of witch stories are hardly based on that. Excavations early this century found goats had lived inside the cave entrance and a milking pot was discovered along with a crystal ball, a comb of antler, a bronze brooch and a sacrificial knife — and the bones of a female. Roman coins lay on top. Was this a legend based on fact?

The museum explains the complexities of Somerset's under-Mendip world and shows some of the prehistoric finds. The remains of woolly rhinoceros, mammoth, reindeer, wild ox, bear, wolf and arctic fox (the bones sometimes with the marks of having been gnawed by hyenas) have all been found in the caves. In 1962 a fox cub slid down fissures connecting to the outside and became marooned in the caves. Vandalism is nothing new — the central cave has the stumps of stalactites because the poet Alexander Pope shot them down so he could place them in his garden at Twickenham. We see three caverns basically but a score of others have been explored. You need a good two hours for caves, museum and mill. You might even be able to tell a stalactite from a stalagmite when you leave.

There is a historical fun fair and a collection of Madame Tussaud's stored heads which may or may not attract, but

Above right *The subterranean River Axe in one of the Wookey Hole caverns.* (Wookey Hole Caves Ltd)

Right *The Paper Mill at Wookey Hole.* (Wookey Hole Caves Ltd)

don't miss a visit to the Mill where the process of creating hand-made paper has been revived. You can see it all, from rags to watermarking to finished work. A mill was established here before 1610 which makes it one of the earliest in England. 'Quick streams and clear water' ensured paper mills spring up at several places along the foot of the Mendips. When lead mining polluted the waters of Wookey Hole it was serious enough for litigation against the mine owners.

Meals, snacks and drinks are available. Hours are 9.30 am–5.30 pm, April–September; 10.30 am–4.30 pm October. Tel: 0749 72243. Wookey Hole Caves Ltd, Wells, Somerset BA5 1BB.

Day 8

A Mendip day

Bart 7   OSLR 182
OSPF ST44/54   ST45/55
8 miles (85) 270 metres (2,280)

'The mysterious fascination of the Mendips is so real and vital to those who know this extraordinary upland that it seems as if the hills are a living entity. In no way do they resemble any other hill range in England.' So wrote Maxwell Frazer in her book *Somerset*, published by the Great Western Railway Company in 1934. It is a book worth ordering in a library to enjoy the many illustrations — and to compare and contrast with the present. On the Mendips little has changed.

Ebbor Gorge to Priddy

Leave Wookey Hole by the Ebbor Farm road. Just past the caves' entrance as the road steepens a sign warns 'This road is not suitable for charabancs'. We turn off at a WMW *Priddy 3* sign. The initial green track can be churned to mud by horses but soon enters the safety of the Nature Reserve woods, from which point the track on is excellent. There is a notice board and the map is worth studying. The limestone formations are the specialists' interest. We are probably glad of the shade of the oaks and ash and the woods are popular with badgers but, being nocturnal, they are seldom seen by walkers. Ebbor Gorge was given to the National Trust by the late Mrs Hodgkinson in 1967 in memory of Sir Winston Churchill.

There is a WMW post, *Priddy 2½*, at steps going off right but ignore this turning for the more interesting track up the gorge. Just 30 yards on the path splits, the left branch leading up to a scenic NT car park on the Wookey Hole–Priddy road, the right leading on up the gorge. The angle suddenly steepens and there is a surrealist atmosphere of ferns and ivy-draped trees and screes, of grey cliffs and misty tree canopies. A brontosarus would seem quite natural! There is no stream for the waters flow underground, just one of the feeders of the River Axe that bursts forth at Wookey Hole. A second steep section is so hemmed in by the crags you can touch both sides at once. A largish tree trunk bars further progress up the gorge — and makes a welcome seat. The main path bears right to climb up the south side of the gorge but we take a smaller track (a notice warns 'No access to car park') up the north side to leave the woods at a stile beside a reserve board.

Over the stile go 20 yards on and cross the fence, right, at wooden railings. The convex slope leaves little view ahead but aim to pass close by the thickest area of scrubby trees visible ahead. Cross a tumbled grey wall (when did we last see a dry-stone wall?) and after a belt gone to bracken and thistles pass the (east) end of a second, isolated, bit of wall. Angle across right to a stile near the apex of the gorge's trees and follow the hollow curve of the next field up near its right edge to reach a stile on to a farm track (Dursdon Drove). We are now truly on the Mendip plateau, a strangely quiet 'other world' with only the 1,000 feet mast on Pen Hill to the east to remind us of the modern high tech world. This mast was built in 1969 and transmits all television channels besides being used by police, ambulance, water, gas, electricity authorities and radio enthusiasts.

Turn right along the rutted track to reach several gates. Cross a stile on the left by another WMW sign *Priddy 1½*. (The WMW has been on a big right-flanker.) Follow along the edge of the field which curves round by a corner fenced off for a stand of trees and 60 yards before the end of the field we swop over to follow the other side of the wall. Repeat the edging in the next field. Cross another stile and aim for the far wall then turn left along the top wall to a stile on to the road half a mile short of Priddy. Turn right and walk along to pretty Priddy. Apart from the corral of a play area opposite the Queen Victoria Inn the village is very pleasant and peaceful.

Priddy Church in the Mendips. Note the typical slab stile in the wall. (Deborah Waller)

Turn left at the crossroads (*Cheddar $6\frac{1}{4}$*). There are two semi-detached cottages on the right, the second of which has a plaque on the wall with a cheery inscription, probably made by the builder:

> This stone my name shall evar
> Have when I hame Dead and laye
> in my grave and Greedy wormes
> my Body eat Then you may read
> my Name compleat.
> Thomas Reeves 1739.

The green lies ahead with the New Inn to the left. The inn may be new but the building dates back to 1477, and provides an excellent lunch spot, inside or out, depending on the weather. On the green there is a sheep market each

The hurdles shelter on Priddy Green.

The Priddy Circles. (Cambridge University Collection of Air Photographs; copyright reserved)

August (Wednesday nearest 21 August) which has been a regular event for 600 years. It was moved out of Wells during the Black Death in 1348 and stayed. The odd thatched construction on the green is a shelter for the hurdles once used at the market. Metal ones are now used but a superstition declares the old hurdles stay: as long as they are on the green the fair will continue.

Priddy is the highest village on the Mendips and was quite an important mining base in Roman times. The Priddy Circles are a collection of Neolithic circles a mile to the north-east which lie in a line and are very impressive, but to see them properly, an aerial view is required. Scores of tumuli litter the fields — over 500 we are told. Those on Priddy's North Hill are often lined-up. Completely absent are streams, because rain water simply soaks into the soil or goes down *swallets* or *slockers* and, as often as not, appears at the foot of the hills. Priddy's rain water drains into the underground Axe which emerges through Wookey Hole. Just where water goes is discovered by pouring in dye to tag the water so to speak. Here, however, the poisonous lead waste flowing down to Wookey and Wells made the stream courses all too well known, and this health hazard was one influence that led to the mines being closed down. The characteristic fields with their limestone walls are relatively new, dating to *c.* 1880. Priddy's St. Cuthbert's lead workings finally closed down in 1908. Blake was writing about Priddy in the lines on 'dark satanic mills' and his vision of a New Jerusalem has come true on Mendip. The mines have gone; now there is a 'green and pleasant land'.

Priddy offers three inns, a couple of B&Bs and a camp site (with café/store) at Townsend (522517), so if you already know Cheddar well it might be tempting to spend the night here and regain tomorrow's route at Charterhouse, one hour's walk to the north-west. The special quality of the Mendips was recognized in 1972 when 84 square miles were declared an Area of Outstanding Natural Beauty.

To Draycott and Cheddar

Leave Priddy by the road along by the New Inn; it climbs up past The Batch, whose houses all seem to be gables-on to

the road. After $\frac{1}{3}$ mile a road comes in right (Dale Lane) an
we take to the fields, left, WMW *Draycott 2$\frac{1}{2}$*. From the gat
head diagonally across, aiming for a gentle saddle in the fiel
ahead, and from there you will see a WMW post ahead at
wall with another stile. Continue across a second field in th
same line to its far apex where fence and wall meet. A stil
leads on to a road. Turn left, for a few hundred yards, to
junction. Our route goes by the gate on the other side
though it is chained and there are no WMW posts for a mil
or two it is still a right of way, ours and for the WMW. (Ther
is a yellow arrow now.)

Follow the left edge of the first field, where there are tw
depressions, typical of limestone areas. From the gate int
the second field aim slightly right of the trees visible over th
crest. There is a stile about 40 yards out from the trees. (4
yards further right you can see a dew pond and a dump
tumulus.) Follow along the line of a fenced area and from it
end angle a bit right across the open field to a yellow-marke
stile 40 yards out from the far right corner of the field. This
and all the stiles to near Draycott, are slab types, well-daube
with yellow paint. Cross the next two fields in line with th
clump of trees with a barn in front of it, then go on alon
beside the trees (a big earthwork in field to left), and almos
before you know it there is suddenly a shock of vie
downwards. The strange limestone landscape of walls an
fields is so self-contained it is easy to forget we've bee
walking up on hills. The drop of Draycott is a reminder!

From the first stile as we begin the descent the next can b
seen at the end of a hedge — where a WMW post appear
again *Draycott $\frac{1}{2}$*. From it a clump of trees and a barn can b
seen down the hill. The route goes down the field to the righ
of these landmarks, by the last of the slab-style stiles. Th
path becomes a green track (briefly) and then a small roa
which leads steeply down into Draycott. The A371
reached at a monument to John Card a local philanthropist.
is made of Aberdeen granite! The plinth is of 'Draycott Ston
a locally quarried pudding stone (conglomerate) the uppe

Above right *The monument to John Card at Draycott.*

Right *The old pump at Draycott.*

band polished like marble to demonstrate that it *could* be polished. The quarries no longer exist. Next to the monument is an old village pump which was last used in the 1970s. The village is mentioned in *Domesday Book*.

Walk along the main road past the Red Lion to a fork. The right fork is ours, School Lane, with St Peter's church on the right. Our road can be followed all the way to Cheddar but just beyond Bradley Cross paths down the fields give a pleasant option for walkers. (The WMW does a rather unnecessary diversion up to Carscliff Farm and down again. There are a large number of strawberry nurseries near Draycott and you could pick up part of supper *en passant*. Draycott still calls its festival a Strawberry Fair and the pub by the old station is Strawberry Special. Somerset is of course also famous for its cider and its cheese (synonymous with Cheddar), and there are plenty of tempting home-made wines, bottled fruits, jams, sweets, local pâtés and so on to satisfy the hungriest of walkers' appetites.

At Bradley Cross the road begins to snake down. At the first bend there is a gate (fine view out to the Levels) with a stile beside it (a line of telegraph poles runs down towards the tower of Cheddar church). Angle across the field, slightly left, to an obvious gate. Descend the next field by the hedge, go through a gate, to continue on down by the wall. This leads to a gate at the top of a lane which

Cheddar Cross.

The cliffs of the Cheddar Gorge.

s followed down to the main road.

There are two camp sites if you turn left, Church Farm, Tel:)934 743048 and Froglands Farm, Tel: 0934 742058, and several B&Bs will be noted, even in the short distance (right) o the restored fourteenth-century market cross. The youth hostel is signposted: along Bath Street and Station Road, hen right along The Hayes and up a narrow lane. Cheddar YH, Hillfield, Cheddar, Somerset BS27 3HN, Tel: 0934 742494. Open every day, March–September, from 5 pm. Evening meal 6.30 pm.

There are plenty of shops and services, hotels and other B&Bs while towards Cheddar Gorge the quiet town becomes a frantic tourist area with endless tea rooms, souvenir shops and so on. There is some accommodation too, as well as another camp site a mile out on the Axbridge side of Cheddar, Broadway House: Tel: 0934 742610. Part of the attraction, as at Wookey Hole, lies underground, but the road itself wends on up the most remarkable gorge in England with towering limestone cliffs rising sheer from the road. An evening wander, with the tourists away and sunset touching the grey rock with warm tones is recommended. Tourist

Gough's Cave Diamond Chamber. (Cheddar Showcaves)

Cheddar Church. (Deborah Waller)

office: Cliff Street, Tel: 0934 744071, (or, winter, Cheddar Library, Union Street, Tel: 0934 742769).

The caves are not to be missed. Gough's Cave and Cox's Cave were discovered in the nineteenth century by gentlemen with those names. Other chambers have been added since. (The Mendips have over 30 miles of known passages!) The many-hued formations are among the most beautiful in the world, not surpassed by the great caves of America or Belgium. There is a museum with archaeological finds from the caves, including the remains of a man, over 10,000 years old. During my *Groats End Walk* I went through the caves and gave them full marks, especially as they allowed my dog to go too! An old tradition claims a dog entered a cave here and was lost, only to appear at Wookey Hole, and the devil was blamed for another 'lost' dog which reappeared shorn of most of its coat. The caves are open every day except Christmas Day. Tel: 0934 742343.

The earliest historical mention of Cheddar is in the will of King Alfred, in 901. Traces of ruins from that period lie in the Kings of Wessex School grounds. In 941 King Edmund is reported to have narrowly escaped falling to his death over the cliffs in the gorge while chasing a stag. *Domesday Book* listed four manors. The Norman de Cheddres family may have financed the magnificent church in 1380, which has an interior unique in being brightly painted (as many once were), quite apart from its store of ancient workmanship. One of Cheddar's worthies was Hannah More who started a school for the poor in 1789. An early woman of character was Sabina Peche who insisted on her rights as Chief Forester of Somerset in the days of Edward I and thought nothing of riding their bounds — and that was Exmoor as well as Mendip. A railway from Bristol in 1869 brought the first tourists. The last train ran in 1969 but the tourists still come. Cars and quarries are the main eyesores in the Mendip Hills.

Cheddar cheese has a recorded history going back 700 years, and it was popular with Henry II and Charles I. Among the many shops and cafés in the Gorge is a cheese factory where you can watch Cheddar cheese being made in Cheddar, and taste it as well. There is also a small confectionery factory, the Cheddar Sweet Kitchen, where handmade sweets are produced. On the non-gastronomic side there are plenty of craft shops: there is a pottery near the caves, and in Union Street is Lennon's, where hand-made jewellery is produced and stones and fossils are for sale; everything, as they proclaim, 'from diamonds to dinosaur dung'.

Day 9

Over the Mendip Hills

Bart 7   OSLR 182, 172
OSPF ST45/55   ST46/56   ST47/5
17 miles (102) 630 metres (2,910)

Mendip crossing

It is quite a long day to Bristol but the walking is varied and interesting, and an early start should allow Blagdon to be

The Cheddar Gorge. (Cambridge University Collection of Air Photographs; copyright reserved)

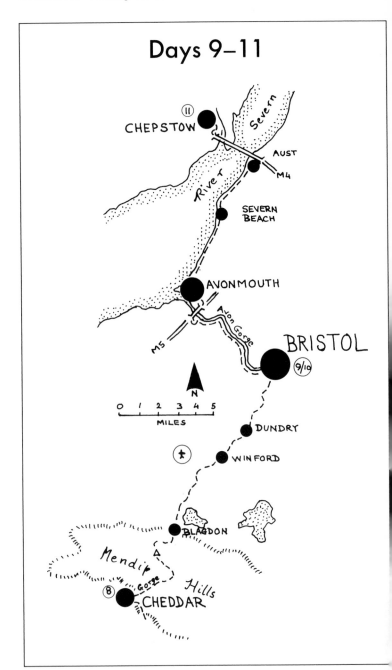

Days 9–11

CHEPSTOW ⑪

Severn

AUST

M4

River

SEVERN BEACH

AVONMOUTH

Avon Gorge

M5

BRISTOL ⑨/⑩

N

0 1 2 3 4 5
MILES

DUNDRY

WINFORD

BLAGDON

Mendip Gorge Hills

⑧ CHEDDAR

reached in time for lunch. Winford is the only other village on the way. (Cheddar–Blagdon $3\frac{1}{2}$ hours, Blagdon–Winford 2 hours, Winford–Bristol $2\frac{1}{2}$ hours, plus refreshment stops, seems reasonable.)

Leave Cheddar by starting off towards the Gorge, passing the Butcher's Arms, crossing the River Yeo (which gushes out of Gough's Cave) and then bearing right up the steep road (**not** St Andrew's Road) through a hamlet called Lippiatt. Turn left at the first junction. After about 100 yards the lane bends right and forks. Take the left fork (briefly) towards the gate of a private house then turn up into the scrubby wood on a footpath. This comes out at a viewing tower, which looks like a lighthouse which has gone astray, above Jacob's Ladder, a line of 274 steps leading up from the Gorge; an alternative start. A fee is charged during 'office hours' but the route is left open otherwise — so an early start saves! The folly tower was built by an eccentric Cheddar baker who finally went 'bonkers' and tried to fly across the Gorge!

From the tower simply follow the track up and along for a

Passing Black Rock on the way to the Mendips. (Graham Cheshire)

mile. There are several spots where you can peer down (as much as 450 feet) into the gorge, the only place in Britain where the Cheddar Pink (*Dianthus caesius*) grows wild. You can also take a last look back to the Somerset Levels which have dominated the history of the region — and our route over the last few days. It is all there, from Glastonbury Tor to Hinkley Point (mystery to mystery), with the Quantocks now mere eyelashes on the horizon.

As height is gained the trees largely peter out (note the battered yews) to be replaced by gorse. A wall is crossed and views back become views forward as the highest point of the cliffs is passed. Follow the path ahead to dip and pass left of a crag, go through some bracken and descend steeply through trees to the road at the head of the Gorge.

Cross the road to the Black Rock Gate (stile) opposite (hail and farewell to WMW posts) which leads into the Black Rock Nature Reserve. There are leaflets on it and the Velvet Bottom Reserve at the information board 50 yards on. You walk up to pass an old limekiln and then pass under the prow of the Black Rock, once a quarry. There are resident rooks and plenty of rabbits. The valley is part of an old drove and becomes quite narrow. Just before the track swings left to go up Long Wood (a less interesting route) we abandon it and cross a stone stile marked by a pole between two field gates on the right. A second stone stile (yellow marker) soon after leads into Velvet Bottom. A series of walls (dams) and level areas are at once curious — the result of lead mining which was carried on here from Roman times to a hundred years ago. No trees grow on the levels as they have a high lead content from long filtering. Circular depressions are 'buddles' where the ore was washed. Later you walk over slag heaps where even a hundred years is not time enough for vegetation to reclothe the poisoned land. Cows and sheep cannot graze here for long periods or they are poisoned, although rabbits don't seem to suffer. Hawthorn (and blackthorn and buckthorn) has to be controlled as it swamps the less-contaminated areas.

The track passes a hut with a big yew tree then the upper Reserve sign before reaching a small tarred road. It comes down, left, from St Hugh's Church and the county's Outdoor Activities Centre, Charterhouse, and runs on to reach Priddy.

Top *Velvet Bottom in the Mendips.* (Graham Cheshire)

Above *The grass snake on the road at Velvet Bottom.*

n big storms in 1968 the road dammed up a lake which eventually washed away a section and swept down into Cheddar. Quite a few Roman artifacts were uncovered as a result!

Turn right along the road, briefly, then go through a gate (left) and continue up the valley: all 'gruffy ground' like a green, tossing sea. The mining peak was the seventeenth century, but the area was gone over again in the mid nineteenth century.

When I joined the road here one dewy September morning nearly stood on a beautiful grass snake. The chill seemed to

Top *Remains of the horizontal flues in the Charterhouse reserve.* (John Holtham)

Above *Beacon Batch trig point on Blackdown, the bleak summit of the Mendips.* (Graham Cheshire)

---

have left it torpid, because I explored and returned and it was still there when I walked on. (Adders are also common on the Mendips.) There is a map board for the Blackmoor Reserve where we turn left (and keeping left again at a fork) to continue up the valley. Approaching the trees we come on a post with footpath signs pointing ahead along the good track, and left on a small footpath. The latter is our route but it is worth going on another hundred yards to see the main site of the ancient lead smelting. There is a long tail of glassy spoil and off right the old condenser flues. These long horizontal flues could run for hundreds of yards before there was the normal high chimney (to create updraught). Lead, being a volatile metal, was cooled in these flues, condensed on their walls and was then scraped off by the workers sent along their tunnel-like lengths. No *Health and Safety at Work Act* in those days!

Return to the guidepost. You can see the path dropping to go over the one-time dam of a settlement pond (now mostly marsh), to a stile and up beside a field to a road. Across the road you can see the square of a Roman settlement — probably built for the miners who worked here. There are plenty of old sites too.

Follow the path across to the road, turn right and, shortly, left up the road (Raines Batch) leading to the wireless masts which show over some trees. Immediately before the wireless station take the track left which is followed for several fields' length in the same line to a gate giving access to the last surviving area of Mendip moorland. The path continues to the trig point of Beacon Batch 325 metres (1,072 feet), the highest point in the Mendip Hills. The Moor is called Blackdown (or Black Down) and with its heather and tumuli it recalls Black Hill on the Quantocks. The heather thrives as the soil is acidic with sandstone capping the Mendip limestone here. Burrington Combe, down to the north-west, is another Somerset spot associated with a hymn. While sheltering from a storm the Reverend Augustus Toplady was inspired to write *Rock of Ages*. The combe also has some caverns and passages which are popular with cavers. Last century a cavern was found with 50 skeletons in it, all neatly laid out as if they had died in their sleep.

Take a path that runs off at right angles to the one by which we came. There are a great many paths to confuse but the required one heads towards the lakes (avoid the larger one with the estuary ahead) which are artificial but attractive. The smoke of Avonmouth can be seen in the distance. The Somerset-Avon boundary is crossed on the descent. Avon was a creation of reorganization in 1974, forming a new

The 'Rock of Ages' in Burrington Combe in the Mendips. (Graham Cheshire)

administrative county from parts of Somerset, Gloucester-shire and the City and County of Bristol — not altogether a welcomed change. Bear right on a descending traverse path which puts Crew Valley Lake ahead. The track then swings left through the fields by an old drove to reach the B3134 at Ellick House Farm. Turn right then left at the first junction (*Blagdon 1, etc*). After 100 yards turn left down the Newfields Drive to the first house. Take the path between its garden and the hedge (overgrown late in the season) to a

128

field which is descended to a gate giving on to a lane (Luvers Lane). Turn right, then through a gate, left, immediately after, to follow down the left edges of two fields and reach a grassy lane at some houses. Follow this, right, back on to the Blagdon road which falls steeply into the village which straggles in sun-catching disorder like a town in Spain. There is a pub where the A368 crosses and there are several shops just down the hill from there. The church at Blagdon was almost entirely rebuilt by W.H. Wills (of tobacco-manufacturing fame) who, in the words of Arthur Mee, 'found an ugly church and left a lovely one'. It is almost restful not to have to study a glut of ancient wonders.

Blagdon to Bristol

Leave Blagdon down Station Road (*Blagdon Lake* ½, *etc*). The Great Western Railway has long gone but the old station has had kindly conversion to a modern house. Below the dam the park has some notable trees and on the lake you may see various ducks, plenty of coots and the occasional great-crested grebe.

The road begins to pull up, is joined by another road from Aldwick, and swings right past rook-noisy Long Wood (Ivy Cottage). We leave it 150 yards on to turn left up a lane

Blagdon Lake.

Blagdon Lake. (Graham Cheshire)

labelled 'Unsuitable for Motors (Blagdon View)'. This track (Sutton Lane) gains sufficient height to give a view over the lake — the last really big hill view of the trip. Butcombe, just below us, is the spot where Butcombe Bitter is brewed. You can buy it at the brewery by the *pin* (4½ gallons), the *firkin* (9 gallons) or the *kilderkin* (18 gallons). Or just have a pint!

Turn right at the end of this good bridleway, along a quiet road and, where it forks, turn right (memorial tree), then left at a T-junction, and right again at another fork. This takes us to the top of the hill (passing Cherry Tree Cottage, left). Look back for the last view of the Mendips. Turn left at the next junction (quarry/dump opposite) and on to a crossroads with a well-laden signpost. A bungalow, Greenway, occupies one corner. Go through the gate in the **opposite** corner. The route ahead, through fields, follows a more or less straight line.

Cross diagonally right (passing between two solitary chestnut trees) to a gate near the top right corner of the field and cut the corner of the next field (40 yards) to a gateway right of a big tree. Take the diagonal across the next field (farm at its left end) to a gate, and again across the next field. Kingdown lies ahead and it is best to aim just left of the big building — there is a stile in the corner beside it. Turn right along the road then, at the junction, bear left (past Checkmate).

Roaring noises off left are probably coming from Bristol Airport at Lulsgate Bottom. The Winford Manor junction is a bit complex but follow the *Winford* signs to progress along Parsonage Lane. Winford is reached at a multiple junction and across the road stands the Prince of Waterloo, with the post office/store just right, opposite the garage.

Just beyond the pub is Dundry Lane (*Dundry 1¾*). Go up this: the last real uphill of the day and of the journey unless you have a hilltop B&B in Bristol. As you pull up there is a smart house, Rock Villa, left, then Elwell Farm, right, after which the hill relents. The route swings right (various tracks

---

Below left *Winford Church.* (Graham Cheshire)

Below right *The intricate crown of the tower of Dundry Church.* (Deborah Waller)

Dundry Cross. (Graham Cheshire)

join in) and then left (Downs Road) by the radio masts. The fine church tower with its fretwork top is an obvious landmark for us. It used to guide sailors heading for Bristol being built by the Merchant Venturers at the end of the fifteenth century for this purpose. The view from the top is as fine as any in Somerset or, to be accurate, Somerset and Avon. Dundry stone built quite a few of the Bristol towers. There's an ancient village cross in the churchyard, and a small pub in the village.

Go down Church Road and turn right at the store, then left immediately beyond, Ham Lane. As immediately, turn right to go down The Steps (all 156 of them) and when these run out go through the stile ahead to skirt down the right side of the field to a stile on to a road.

Turn left along it (Oxleaze Lane) to a junction where you turn right. A first glimpse of the Clifton Suspension Bridge gives an impressive idea of its scale. Follow down this road

(Highridge Road) for $\frac{2}{3}$ mile as it flanks a green dome, The Peart (132m). There are some houses, left (Oaktree Gardens), then the road swings right but walkers can keep straight on over the Highridge Common to the road beyond (564685).

Cross this to Sandburrows Road and walk right down its length to a busy meeting of roads (572690). Turn along left to use the pedestrian crossing and down between Bishopsworth Library and the row of shops. Immediately after the toilets and before the Crossways Tabernacle turn down a track, through a stile and a path leads on for over half a mile through a reclaimed 'park' which has taken the name of the stream, The Malago.

When you leave it turn left (and off Sheet 182) along Vale Lane, which swings right to join a busy road. Turn left along this for a quarter of a mile (Parson Street) to a big crossroads with traffic lights and 'No Entry ahead for vehicles'. (I walked into the city in the going-home rush and was very glad to be on foot!) Cross to turn down Bedminster Road (school) and cross over to the shops on the other side (pillar-box). Take the first left beyond these up Shepton Walk, cross over the railway by a footbridge and go straight ahead (Bartletts Road) to reach a main road.

Turn **left** and then take the second road right, Chessel Street. You pass two churches on it and, at the end, turn right. After 100 yards you reach a bigger road. Cross the zebra crossing, turn left, and then first right, Greville Road. When Greville Road swings right we turn left down Upton Road to cross Raleigh Road into a redbrick canyon of redundant tobacco factories. Turn right at the next road, Greenway Bush Lane. This swings left (big block of flats right) and with an unexpected rise brings you on to Coronation Road and the River Avon. Urban Bristol wasn't so bad, was it?

Cross the road (pedestrian crossing) and go over the footbridge across the New Cut of the River Avon, a man-made trench cut through soil and rock to re-route the River Avon. This lands one on Cumberland Road from where most places we want can be reached fairly easily.

About a quarter of a mile west along Cumberland Road is Bristol's only camp site, a small Caravan Club site that is

Above left *SS* Great Britain *in her Bristol home.* (SS *Great Britain*/Maritime Heritage Centre)

Above right *St Mary Redcliffe, Bristol, from the Floating Harbour.* (Graham Cheshire)

always heavily booked. You would have to book weeks rather than days, ahead to ensure a place. The youth hostel or B&B might be simpler. Baltic Wharf Caravan Park at least has a tang of sea to its name. Tel: 0272 268030.

For the town centre, turn east, right, from the footbridge to walk along Cumberland Road for about a quarter of a mile then turn left up Gas Ferry Road (*SS Great Britain* signs) to where this historic ship is berthed. There is a café as well to refresh you before you have a look at Brunel's maritime showpiece. (The route into town continues along the waterside to cross at the first bridge; the next few paragraphs simply describe things to see on the way).

Isambard Kingdom Brunel's SS *Great Britain* was the world's first ship to be built of iron and driven by a screw propeller. Launched in 1843, from the same dock where she is now being restored, she crossed the Atlantic in 1845. Later she spent 25 years carrying thousands of passengers to

Australia, voyages interrupted by troopship work in connection with the Indian Mutiny and the Crimean War. She ended, sadly, as a storage hulk in Port Stanley in the Falkland Islands. However, she was towed 'home' in 1970 and is now one of Bristol's great showpieces.

The entrance is via the Maritime Heritage Centre, which is a sort of glorified ships-and-seas museum with many Bristol connections. Open 10 am–6 pm daily. Tel: 0272 260650. There is also a café and a ferry pick-up point; if leg-weary you can always go by launch up to the centre of the city and come back tomorrow to resume the walk. However, there are other things to see alongside the Floating Harbour — a name that perhaps needs explaining.

The tremendous tidal range in the Severn and Avon meant that for many hours each day ships had to sit on the mud at the quayside. The ingenious solution to this problem was to build locks at either end of a two-mile reach of the river and cut a new channel for the tidal waters, in 1809. This made the oddly-worded Floating Harbour. We came over the cutting to reach Cumberland Road and heading west tomorrow will be able to see the seaward-end locks. The commercial use of the harbour has largely ceased (it is all container traffic to Avonmouth now), but the Floating Harbour has become a great pleasure source for the city — amazing when one recalls the dereliction of just 20 years ago. Making the Floating Harbour cost £600,000 (the estimate was £200,000) so at today's prices it would be astronomic. Even then the growing size of ships was starting the decline of Bristol as a port, because the larger ships could not navigate the tight bends of the river.

Continuing along the wharfs eastwards odd rolling stock indicates the Bristol Industrial Museum which has everything from ancient lorries to a mock-up cockpit of Concorde. Open: Saturday–Wednesday 10 am–12 noon and 1–5 pm. Tel: 0272 99771. The Fairbairn Steam Crane (1875) on the dockside is a scheduled Ancient Monument! Next door is the National Lifeboat Museum, the only one of its kind. Open daily, April–October.

The Tourist Office can supply a map-guide *Bristol: Historic Harbour* which it would be worth obtaining in advance as so much of this lies on our route. (Other useful literature is

135

mentioned at the start of tomorrow's activities.)

Turn left over the Prince Street swing bridge (the spire off to the right is that of St Mary Redcliffe, of which more later), left again once over the bridge to keep following the water, then right at the Arnolfini Building. The youth hostel is beside it, facing the wharf. On the other side the red-daubed *Locheil* is a floating Inn and the buildings along from her are part of the Watershed exhibition area. I once sailed from Oban in the beautiful tall ship *Eye of the Wind* which became the showpiece of the Wine Festival here. There were two tall ships here when I passed in 1983, one being the ill-fated *Marques*, built in Spain *c.* 1917 and rigged as the *Beagle* for the BBC series on Charles Darwin. In 1984, while taking part in the Bermuda-Halifax leg of a Tall Ships' race, she was overwhelmed by a freak squall and went down in about a minute. Last year there were several old ships and the Floating Harbour had a superb atmosphere — an impressive success story.

Bristol certainly has made an effort to use areas which are often urban wastes: the Bristol fashion tradition. When we do things 'on the nail' we are also referring to an old Bristol custom of sealing market bargains, and the nails stand along Corn Street to this day.

The Tourist Information Office is just along a bit at 14 Narrow Quay, Bristol BS1 4QA, Tel: 0272 260767. Before the trip begins it would be advisable to get in touch and obtain their current *Accommodation Guide* and any other guides or information (see tomorrow's ideas). Most B&Bs tend to be uphill north of the river in the Clifton-Cotham-Redland area. There are 30 pages of listed accommodation and plenty not listed so there is no lack. The Publicity and Information Office of the City Council, Tel: 0272 260768, is an alternative source of information.

The youth hostel (opened 1989) is part of the Bristol Centre which the YH Handbook calls a 'new and exciting project'. Sited in one of the Edwardian warehouses, next door to the Arnolfini Arts Centre, it has been turned into a multi-purpose residential study centre but, for our purposes, the hostel is open all day, every day, provides a cafeteria meals service from 8 am to 8 pm and small, semi-private rooms instead of the usual dormitories. Hayman House, 64

Prince Street, Bristol BS2 4HU, Tel: 0272 221659.

This seaworld welcome to Bristol is quite appropriate for Bristol's whole history is connected with exploration and trade overseas. Wines from Bordeaux and Spain have been imported for hundreds of years and the city still hosts the annual (July) World Wine Festival. Thackeray's novel *The Virginians* points to another long trading link, a transatlantic trade that continues to this day: grain, foodstuffs, tobacco being major imports. (Bristol, in 1792, had the first American consulate in Europe.) The city had an early association with flying and in 1969 began the production of Concorde. The Floating Harbour, each June, is the setting for the Powerboat Grand Prix which attracts thousands of visitors. You have been warned.

At the time of the Domesday survey Bristol was already the fourth largest town in England and over the centuries it remained a busy port. The Cabots' voyage of 1497 was a landmark of international importance. By Royal Charter in the time of Edward VI the Society of Merchant Venturers was incorporated. Vessels sailed to Newfoundland with pottery, textiles, furniture, etc. which were traded for fish which was taken to Spain and Portugal and traded for wine. Bristol Cream Sherry is a reminder of this trade. The slave trade is one the city would rather forget about. Slaves, bought in West Africa, were shipped to the West Indies and traded for rum, sugar and tobacco. One privateer returned with a castaway, Alexander Selkirk, who served Defoe as his model for *Robinson Crusoe*. Candlesticks (1712) in the cathedral commemorate this rescue.

In the Civil War Prince Rupert seized Bristol which became the Royalists' centre in the West but Fairfax eventually stormed it. Sons of Bristol include the painter Thomas Lawrence, the 'sailors' friend' Samuel Plimsoll, and the bearded cricketer W.G. Grace.

Day 10

Exploring Bristol

Bart 7   OSLR 172
OSPF ST47/57   ST67/77

The best maps for exploring will probably be local ones from the Tourist Information Centre, Colston Street, Tel: 0272 293891.

Bristol fashion

Bristol, with a population approaching half a million is a big and busy city yet it retains a heart which is small and easily explored on foot. You really need many days to see things properly so make use of the one day available by stocking up with the relevant literature in advance and have your personal priority choices ready. Of course there is no reason why you should not take further days to explore Bristol. Betjeman declared, 'There is no city in England with so much character.'

The Bristol Heritage Walk is a marked trail which takes in many of the historic buildings in the city. There is a guide booklet which details the 39 places to see — and rather optimistically suggests this is a two-hour round, which it may be, just walking, but several of the places to visit could take two hours in themselves. However, the booklet (and the trail) gives a good track to follow along with any diversions to other chosen sites not directly *en route*. The walk follows an anti-clockwise direction and below I list the main attractions of the city in a similar direction. They may or may not be included in the guide. There is only room for the briefest descriptions and it is assumed you'll have provided yourself

The statue of Neptune in front of the Watershed Exhibition Centre. It is Bristol's oldest statue of note. (Above, Graham Cheshire; below Deborah Waller)

with the relevant literature. The numbers relate to the Heritage Walk. Opening times are not given as these are on all the leaflets and booklets available.

Bristol, Historic Harbour has been mentioned. A similar map-guide *Museums and Churches in Bristol* is worth ordering. *The Official Visitors' Guide* is also useful as might be the *Accommodation Guide* and the monthly *Bristol Bulletin* (which lists 'What's On'). The Avon Walkway follows the River Avon up to Bath and there are trail leaflets and a guide to the industrial archaeology of the Avon Valley. You might like to do something like this for an extra day, or even take another to explore Bath, too. What's the hurry? I've picked up all these items from the Tourist Office but titles do change so it would be worth giving the office a ring to ensure you find them or their equivalent **before** you reach Bristol. There won't be time then! Bryan Little's book *The City and Country of Bristol* was one I enjoyed reading after the trip.

Our whistle-stop noting of Bristol landmarks starts at the Centre. Here is the much loved 1723 lead statue of Neptune (1). It was moved to this quayhead site in 1949. The Centre and Colston Avenue were docks until last century, and plaques record some of the famous voyages made from Bristol over the centuries. Walk down by the harbour to the Arnolfini Gallery (2). In a reconstructed warehouse this is an enterprising exhibition centre (noted for modern art) with cinema, bookshop and restaurant. The statue outside is to John Cabot, the sailor-adventurer who (if you discount the Vikings) discovered mainland America. East lies Queen Square (4). The queen was Ann, who visited Bristol in 1702. In the Reform Act Riots of 1831 half the square went up in flames.

Crossing the Floating Harbour brings one to Bristol's most famous church, St Mary Redcliffe. This big building with a spire 285 feet high was largely built in the fourteenth century and is as big and sumptuous as many a cathedral. The hexagonal North porch is unusual. There are many Bristol-associated monuments inside. Southey and Coleridge were married, to sisters, in St Mary's. Every guide book quotes Queen Elizabeth's commendation of the church. One of the oddest connections is with Thomas Chatterton, who began

The striking Cabot statue. (Deborah Waller)

to write poems while at Colston's Hospital (school). He wrote poems and then correspondence which he claimed to have found in a chest in the muniment room of St Mary's. These 'Rowley' poems were published in 1777, seven years after he had committed suicide after moving to London and their forgery, rather like Macphersian's *Ossian*, created a century of controversy about 'the boy poet'. Keats dedicated *Endymion* to the fictional Rowley!

East again is the huge Old Station; closed in 1965 but being restored, it is the oldest surviving major rail terminal and was designed by Brunel. Temple Meads is the present railway station. Back to Queen Square and on to King Street (5). Laid out in 1663 and still lined with historic buildings, including the Theatre Royal (which opened in 1766 and is reputedly haunted by Sarah Siddons), an old almshouse and several pubs, including the historic Llandoger Trow (named from the sailing barges that once plied between Bristol and Wales). Welsh Back (7) is part of the original harbour when the Avon was tidal. A lightship moored at the quay is now a restaurant.

Upstream is Bristol Bridge from which the city derives its name: Bricgstow, the settlement by the bridge. The original

The Elephant, Bristol. (Deborah Waller)

timber bridge was rebuilt in stone in the thirteenth century but the foundations were retained for the present bridge of 1768, the Victorians added the iron extensions. Beyond lies the Castle Park, the twelfth-century castle occupied 11 acres but was demolished on the orders of Cromwell. This was the heart of old Bristol but much of it was destroyed in the bombing raids of 1940. Across the bridge is the Temple

'On the nail' was once meant literally — the nails still stand on which deals were signed in bygone trading days. (John Holtham)

Church, perpendicular in style but with its tower 5 feet out o'
the vertical (since 1400). It is an old Knights Templar Church
but was severely damaged by wartime bombs. On the wes
bank, facing the bridge, St Nicholas Church (9), which was
also gutted, has been turned into an award-winning museum
and brass-rubbing centre. (The painting of *Cabot's Departure
for the New World* was a schoolboy memory which I came
face to face with in its colourful reality.)

Nearby are the fish market (8) (note the decor of the pub
The Elephant), the covered market (10) and All Saint's
Church (11), which brings us to Corn Street where four of the
'nails' still stand outside the Exchange.

Corn Street (12) was the commercial centre of the city
The old High Cross (now at Stourhead in Wiltshire) once
stood at the meeting of Corn Street, Wine Street, High Stree
and Broad Street. Cottle's bookshop was popular with

The equestrian statue of John Wesley. (John Holtham)

eighteenth-century literary figures, Cottle encouraging both Southey and Coleridge while, in his parlour, Wordsworth wrote *Lines Written Above Tintern Abbey*. Southey was born in Wine Street and christened in Christchurch (13). Quarter jacks on the clock strike bells — a reminder of the clock at Wells. Several buildings of interest are pointed out on Broad Street which ends at St John's Gate (16), the only surviving medieval gateway. A church squats on top of it! Turning right from the gate along Nelson Street and the Horsefair takes one to the New Room, the first Methodist church, opened in 1739. There's a fine equestrian statue of John Wesley in the courtyard.

St John's Gate leads us out to the busy sweep of modern traffic on the continuation of the Centre, Colston Avenue. The River Frome still runs here, but underground. Along, left, s the soaring tower of St Stephen's Church, rebuilt in the 1470s by a merchant-mayor. The delicate Gloucestershire-style 'crown' is the only example in Bristol. Across the broad road is the very fine Lewin's Mead Unitarian Chapel (18). Turn up the Christmas Steps (20) which date from 1669. On the left is the Chapel of the Three Kings of Cologne (21) built n the 1480s by a merchant-mayor who had obviously travelled up the Rhine. The three statues of the kings in the niches are modern (1967), the work of Ernest Pascoe. Cross to head up Park Row to the Red Lodge (22) which has a plain exterior but a rich period museum inside. Further along Park Row one comes to the University buildings and the City Museum and Art Gallery (24). The latter could easily gobble up hours, being the grandest museum in south-west England, strong in archaeology and natural history, ceramics and glass. Perhaps its rarest item is Cranach's portrait of *Martin Luther.* The University Tower holds a 10 ton bell, the Great George (23). The refectory (25) was inspired by the Doge's Palace in Venice. Those interested in modern architecture might like to walk on to Clifton to see the striking Roman Catholic Cathedral of SS Peter and Paul which was consecrated in 1973. Even Prince Charles would approve!

The Heritage Walk heads off to Berkley Square (26) and Brandon Hill with the Cabot Tower (27) and Civil War earthworks (28), but we'd better save some time and head down Park Street (33). I invariably come to grief, however as

Above left *The striking front of Bristol Museum.* (City of Bristol Museum and Art Gallery)

Left *A dramatic display in the Natural History section of the Bristol Museum.* (City of Bristol Museum and Art Gallery)

Above *Striking modern sculptures on the gable of the Chapel of Three Kings.* (Deborah Waller)

George's, occupying six numbers, is the largest bookshop in the south-west and any time saved is soon spent there. Great George Street (31) has imposing mansions from the eighteenth and nineteenth centuries and The Georgian House, No 7 (32) has been made into a museum showpiece of that period. St George's Church opposite has been turned into a concert hall because of its excellent acoustics. College Green at the foot of Park Street is

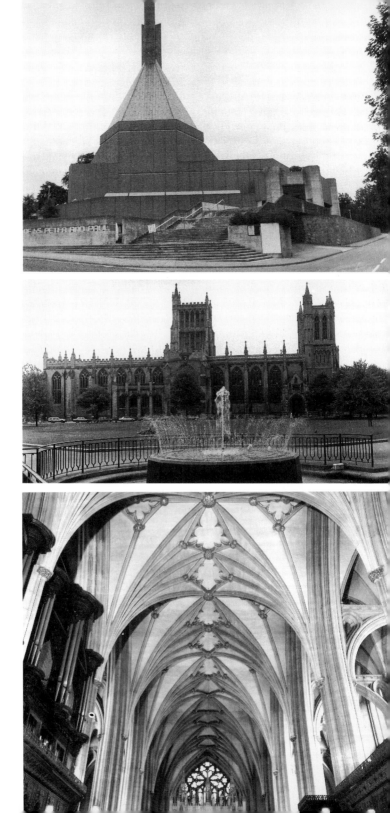

our next area of outstanding human interest.

The Green is dominated by the sweep of the imposing, rather than beautiful Council House (34) (opened by the Queen in 1956) and looks across to the robust rectangular strength of the Cathedral. North of the Green is the Lord Mayor's Chapel, a remnant from the thirteenth-century Hospital of the Gaunts. The interior is beautiful, so don't overlook this unique civic church.

Bristol Cathedral (37) was originally founded in 1140 as an Augustinian monastery. The original Norman archway of its entrance lies just west of the present cathedral — which was only completed in its present form in 1888. St Augustine is reputed to have met the Celtic church leaders here in the early seventh century to try and create a uniform order in the church. Aust also claims to be the site of this meeting, which failed (temporarily) in its aims. The Chapter House is one of the finest Norman rooms in the country and the choir is unusually rich. In 1539 the Abbey was dissolved and the nave was destroyed and built over, then in 1542 the buildings became the new Cathedral. In 1868 work began to rebuild the nave, which was opened 10 years later, and several additions have been made since to this brave building. The interior is tremendous, the best of all the day's sights/sites.

The cathedral offers refreshments and there is a shop. Resting one's legs is usually welcome, since Bristol gives quite the hardest day of our walk! There is a Bristol entry in Kilvert's *Diary* (4 June 1874) which is a nice cameo. The parson was in a confectioner's off College Green eating a bun when a ragged, barefoot girl attracted his attention. Her wistful look of hunger was 'irresistible' — so she got a bun as well. Walking down from the Green to the Centre we pass a Jubilee statue of Queen Victoria. The Centre's garden has

---

Top left   *The Roman Catholic Cathedral Church of Saints Peter and Paul, Bristol.* (John Holtham)

Middle left   *Bristol Cathedral.*

Bottom left   *The ceiling of the choir, Bristol Cathedral.* (Bristol Cathedral Trust)

another figure standing on a pedestal. This turns out to be Burke, who looks as if he was bowling right arm round the wicket. Neptune is quite unimpressed.

Bristol is a city of statues. Some have been mentioned already but also worth seeing in Broad Quay is the striking figure of Isambard Kingdom Brunel. Back at the hostel on Narrow Quay, is the Cabot figure, looking as if he were alive and about to leap into a ship and sail to distant dreams. I think that is my favourite.

Bristol's tribute to Brunel. (Deborah Waller)

Day 11

Avon and Severn

Bart 7   OSLR 172
OSPF ST47/57   ST48/58
20 miles (122) 100 metres (3,010)

Down the River Avon

Most walkers should make Chepstow in one day but it is possible to break the journey at Severn Beach by camping there or catching a train back to Bristol (the option of a day without a rucksack). The day falls into three parts: the walk down the Avon, the industrial miles of Avonmouth and beyond, and the quieter walk to the Severn Bridge to Chepstow, Wales and the start of the Offa's Dyke path. It is still quite a way to John o' Groats!

The day starts by returning along Cumberland Road to the footbridge over the New Cut of the River Avon. If coming from The Centre or the youth hostel why not take a harbour ferry along to the Maritime Heritage Centre and pick up the walk there? You have an enjoyable and different look at Bristol from a boat. You can also look for Plimsoll lines on the ships you pass. (Sam Plimsoll was born in Bristol.)

Return to the footbridge, ascend it and come down again on to the pathway westwards that runs between the railway and the river. Periodically on the River Avon miles you may see the AV marks of the Avon Walkway or the green discs of Cyclebag, for our route generally follows a path which runs from east of Bath to Avonmouth, and a more local cycle trail. In practice signs can be missing, or these ways go on peculiar diversions, so I perforce give detailed descriptions occasionally on a walk which basically follows the left bank of

Left *The Clifton Suspension Bridge and the Avon Gorge from the air.* (Cambridge University Collection of Air Photographs; copyright reserved)

Above *Clifton Suspension Bridge from the River Avon.* (Graham Cheshire)

he River Avon on its seaward journey.

Walk along from the footbridge until you come to the next bridge, a railway bridge which is sometimes not shown on maps, but which we cross (quite legally), then turn right along by some chestnut trees to pass under the big new road bridge — and there ahead, above, is the splendid Clifton Suspension Bridge, Brunel's greatest achievement which he never saw himself as he died in 1859 and the bridge was only completed in 1864. The 702 feet span is 245 feet above high water level. Aircraft have flown under the bridge and jumping off it, with both sporting or suicidal intentions, is not uncommon practice. A jilted lover leapt over in 1885 but her petticoats acted like a parachute and she landed, uninjured, in the mud. She lived to be 85.

Before reaching the Gorge look back from the end of the park, if the tide is out, to see the locks of the Floating Harbour. (Later on be sure to look **back** to the bridge). The Gorge is limestone and very similar really to the Cheddar Gorge.

For the next hour or so the only instruction needed is

Top   *Taking the ferry down the Floating Harbour.*

Above   *The hamlet of Pill, once full of pilot cutters, now bed.
pleasure craft.*

'Follow the river'. After a big loop there is a creek which
diverts us off the river to skirt a couple of fields round Chape
Pill Farm to debouch on to the drive out from this attractiv

building. We pass a secretive reservoir, set among big trees, before the road pulls up and along to a roundabout at the entrance to Ham Green Hospital. On the right the grounds of a big house have cedars and other fine trees (noisy with coal its last time I passed) and on the left is a splendid full-sized variegated sycamore, a tulip tree and other fine specimens. Go straight on at the roundabout.

Take the first road right (between hedges, before the playing field) and at its end is the Regional Infectious Diseases Unit. To the left is an Avon Walkway post directing us along outside the wired area. ('Danger. Infected Area. Keep Out.') Cross a stile and pass a trough to skirt the last of the hospital area. There is a clear view to the Avonmouth Bridge up ahead, while below lies the odd village of Pill, red roofs crowding down to a creek. Descend to a stile to pass beside some houses (Public footpath sign), then bear left to come out at the inlet. Walk towards the red brick railway bridge but before reaching it you can skirt round the creek by some grass edged with bollards. (If there is a wind the halyards on the yachts will be tapping out their rhythm.) The official Walkway goes off on a convoluted tour but it is simpler to follow the river. Pill at one time was the base for pilots operating on the River Avon and the Severn Estuary. Bristol pilot cutters were graceful adn a few still exist as treasured museum pieces. Tilman's *Mischief* was a Bristol cutter and so was his last love, *Baroque*, which is still sailing. Pill has several shops, pubs and other services if so required.

The Duke of Cornwall pub stands on the corner beyond the inlet, looking on to Pump Square, which we cross to go along Marine Parade, tight by the river, and when grass banks run down to the water/mud we swing left to pass behind a row of houses. This street swings left to a T-junction where we turn right along Avon Road. At a fork turn left towards a bridge under the railway, but bear right before reaching the bridge, on to a track with cycle and Shirehampton walking signs. This takes you to the M5.

Strictly speaking the footpath over the M5 bridge is on the west, seaward, side and is reached by a path going right and under the M5 and then up, steps eventually, to gain the walkway. The nearer east side is for cyclists, etc, but seems to be the one taken by all and sundry. Either side you have

the M5 for company for a mile and it introduces several miles of what is claimed to be the most intensely industrialized area in Britain. It has a strange fascination. You can find oxygen again on the Severn Bridge and gargle before going to bed in Chepstow.

Crossing the bridge Shirehampton lies on the right and Avonmouth on the left. If the pollution is not too bad you may just make out the Severn Bridge. Whichever side you have crossed when you descend off the M5 to a minor dual carriageway (B4054), turn left, and cross the road to use a pedestrian underpass at a busy roundabout. Follow signs for Avonmouth A4, and Severn Beach A403.

Along Severn shores

You can amuse yourself on the way to Severn Beach by listing all the firms or industries you observe. There are huge docks (the tidal range is 40 feet!), fuel depots, smelting and chemical works, a fertilizer plant, cold stores, gas works, mills and factories. On my *Groats End Walk* trip I came through it before dawn when that area was all lit up. It was like something out of science fiction.

After a quarter of a mile the main road swings right in an area of shops, cafés, pubs, etc, (*Severn Beach/Aust A403*) and heads off on a long, long straight marked by variously coloured plumes of smoke. After a generous mile the road bends right over a level-crossing (the left fork leads in to a fuel depot) and half a mile on the A403 bridges another railway to bend hard right at the Chittening industrial estate.

At present we are forced to follow the road round on this diversion and there is little pavement or grass verge to walk on. Each elbow of the road is followed by another level-

Top left   *The motorway bridge over the Avon — the start of the industrialized world of Avonmouth.*

Middle left   *The 'other world' of Avonmouth ...* (Cambridge University Collection of Air Photographs; copyright reserved)

Bottom left   *... an extraordinary contrast to the rural Somerset and Avon walk.* (Graham Cheshire)

crossing (not used so they could vanish when the road is resurfaced). The authorities hope to revive the right of way running **behind** the industrial complex so if this is available it gives the obvious first choice. Look out for footpath signs.

When the road swings back right parallel with the railway and estuary you could force a way along between road and railway (Chittening Warth on map) but the road verges are now wide and easier underfoot. At the *Bristol* city/county sign there is a footpath sign, left. Follow this and the acrid air and industrial squalor soon fades away.

The footpath runs along and then crosses the railway beyond a tidal drain. At the stile I spotted an owl beating along and stood still. The bird was so intent on its mousing that it passed only three yards from me. Gulls and rare eiders called from the sea, there were starlings, pigeons, larks, a wren, several warblers, thrushes, blackbirds and some magpies, yet over the road from this path by the railway track was a chemical works.

The path becomes a road after some pipes run to the sea (soft verges) and when this bends right under the railway it is easy to walk on by the sea wall into Severn Beach. Turn right at the start of the promenade if wanting the hamlet's facilities (several shops), otherwise keep along the coast for the bridge.

Severn Beach was once a holiday resort beside the Severn ferry so had a period of decline, which seems to be passing as its proximity to cities, towns and bridge makes a seaside home desirable. There are two well-appointed camp sites. Pilning seems surrounded by pubs but none offers accommodation.

Strong walkers will have planned to reach Chepstow with its youth hostel and ample accommodation of all standards but if seven more miles seems too much the best answer is to catch a train from Severn Beach back to Bristol. There are about six trains between 16.45 and 22.10. If you had a B&B in the Clifton-Redland-Montpelier areas of Bristol (where there are stations on this line) you could plan this in advance booking in for two nights, and having an easier day without a rucksack. Accommodation at Avonmouth is largely limited to transport drivers and commercial users. There are nine trains in the morning back to Severn Beach — starting at 05.15

There is no Sunday service. Bristol Information Office has timetables, or apply to British Rail.

If simply walking through Severn Beach, keep to the promenade and on along The Binn Wall. Under your feet at one stage is the railway tunnel (Britain's longest at about $4\frac{1}{2}$ miles) that passes under the Bristol Channel, linking London and South Wales. Built in 1873–86 by a pupil of Brunel it runs as deep as 100 feet below the seabed. A wired-off area is the top of one of the ventilation shafts. New Passage, as the name suggests, is a one-time ferry terminal.

Back in Civil War times a Welsh ferryman came across to and some Royalists he was happy to help escape. On his return, however, he met the pursuit who forced him, at sword point, to carry them across to the English side. They leapt ashore at the first opportunity and the Royalist boatman pulled away with a cheery heart. He had landed them on the English Stones, those tidal reefs that lie off Severn Beach! I wonder if he was paid for his services?

There are good views of the Severn Bridge. Pass through a stile and along a banktop path round to a sluice/bridge over the river. Cross this and continue on towards the New Passage Rifle Range. If red flags are flying a sentry will politely indicate a diversion inland to avoid the sea wall. A notice gives dates of use; pretty well every weekend, never on Monday, Tuesday and only sometimes on the other days. The firing always starts at 9 am so campers should aim to be through by then. From the warning notice turn right to a bridge (you can see a white notice on it) then upstream to cross back by another. Turn right along telephone poles behind the buildings and go right round the perimeter — well signposted in red. The walking is on grass. Once back on the sea wall it is a mile along to the B4055.

A stile leads on to this at Cake Pill Gout. Turn left and follow the road. There used to be posts on the verge marked (in feet!) to show the depth of water on the road. It is possible to walk along on grass on either side of the road to the Old Passage (the ferry before the ferry before the bridge was built). Here you pull up for Aust and cross the first contour line since the River Avon. Just before the A403 and Aust village there is a bridge sign saying 'Pedestrians, prams and dogs on leads only' — which rather reduces us to the ranks

Above left   *The Severn Bridge.* (Cambridge University Collection of Air Photographs; copyright reserved)

Above right   *A striking view of the Severn Bridge.* (Graham Cheshire)

— and indicates our way to Chepstow, still four miles away, half of that being a bridge which we cross on the seaward side. Aust is a quiet hamlet. There is a camp site at the pub (meals) and little else and a scenic motorway service centre over on the north side of the M4. From here we set out to cross the River Severn, a river over a mile wide and with one of the largest tidal ranges in the world — up to 46 feet. Tides can run at 9 knots. The Severn Bridge is a spectacular way to finish our walk.

The Bridge was opened by the Queen in 1966, after being five years abuilding. The towers rise to 400 feet, and the main span of 3,240 feet made it the seventh largest in the world at the time. The side spans are 1,000 feet. The bridge not only crosses the huge River Severn but also strides over the Beachley point to bridge the River Wye. The Wye main

Wales at last! The tranquil setting of Chepstow Castle on the River Wye.

span is 770 feet with side spans of 285 feet. The stayed-girder form is applying the cantilever principle in cable form, the first-ever such. A lot of novel ideas were incorporated in the bridge: the suspension cables are not vertical but inclined to give extra strength and rigidity. The roadway is made of hollow box sections for lightness. All was, of course, thoroughly tested and the bridge regarded as the finest construction of the century. Ah well... Welcome to Wales, if you've survived the noise, the trembling and the road works on the bridge!

Chepstow

Once across the bridge follow the public footpath signs down then turn right through a tunnel under the motorway. Follow this road up for a mile until it meets the A48 (Thornwell Road) on a nasty hill with blind corners so the pedestrian is glad to

have a safe pavement. Turn right for the town centre. There
is a wide range of accommodation available, quite a bit of i'
on the road down to the castle. The Tourist Informatior
Office, The Gate House, High Street has an up-to-date
accommodation list, etc. There are local and long-distance
bus services and a railway station. Or you can continue on to
do Offa's Dyke as well! The camp site (547922) is south o'
Offa's Dyke away on the other side of the River Wye but a
half-hourly bus service to Beachley passes it.

For the youth hostel also turn right out of Thornwell Road
but cross the road immediately (and carefully!) to go up a
lane to bear left (Hardwick Hill Lane), then right (Vauxhall
Lane). After the Ambulance Station turn right and ther
almost at once left. Follow this road (not named but it is
Mounton Road) across the A466 (*Mounton 1*) and the youth

Below *The beautiful Rennie bridge over the River Wye a*
Chepstow. (Graham Cheshire)

Right *Chepstow Castle from the Rennie Bridge.* (Graham
Cheshire)

Below right *The castle with the towers of the Severn Bridge*
behind. (Graham Cheshire)

hostel is 300 yards along, opposite the Burns Unit of the Mount Pleasant Hospital. Mounton Road, in the opposite direction, is the way in to Chepstow from the hostel. In the eighteenth century the hostel was the home of the Sheriff of Monmouth. Chepstow YH, Mounton Road, Chepstow, Gwent NP6 6AA, Tel: 0291 622685. Open daily, March–31 October (but closed 2–17 September), evening meal 6.30 pm.

Chepstow has its castle which, to me, is the most aesthetic spot to end our linking walk. Chepstow is a great contrast to Minehead though both, at one time, were considerable ports. Chepstow is the Saxon for Market Place (held now in Beaufort Square), but when the conquering Normans arrived, just a year or two after the Battle of Hastings, they called it Striguil. Before that the Romans had a ford, just upstream of the castle, leading to their border town (now Caerleon) and if defence/penetration of the Welsh Marches was the reason for Chepstow's growth, being the lowest bridging point made it possible. History is subtly influenced by geography in a way that is seldom acknowledged.

The newly created Earl of Hereford established the castle here and, by building in stone from the start, has given us one of Europe's oldest surviving stone castles. Hereford fell foul of the king then, 40 years later, the powerful Clare family held it, both as the focal point of Gwent and the port from which they made their Irish conquests. It passed, by marriage, to the powerful Earl of Pembroke and he and his successors built the massive curtain walls, the lower bailey with its massive gatehouse and several of the towers. Marriage again took the castle to a new family, the Bigods, Earls of Norfolk, who did much building including having the town encircled by a wall, much of which survives today. Known as the Port Wall a good section of it can be seen in the Dell when looking from the castle battlements. The town gate was rebuilt in 1524 and then used as a prison. Henry VII abolished the Marcher Lordships and Monmouth was made the head of the new county, but Chepstow kept its importance as a port right up to the nineteenth century when the growth of Newport, Cardiff and Bristol eclipsed it.

The railway bridge was built by Brunel during 1849–52 with a main span of 300 feet, the weight of which was carried by two huge tubes — an idea well ahead of its time and echoed in the box construction of the Severn Bridge roadway. Brunel used the high rise of the tide to help place the tubes, and this was repeated in the Severn Bridge construction where the box sections, built at Fairfields Yard, were floated down the Wye to the bridge. Brunel's bridge was completely reconstructed in 1962 but still keeping its character is the graceful road bridge built by John Rennie in 1816, one of the first cast iron bridges in the world. From it one has an excellent view of the castle which must occupy one of the most spectacular sites in the country, its towers and walls topping a grey limestone cliff above the sweep of the River Wye. An unimaginative concrete bridge, just downstream of the Rennie bridge, is new but hardly likely to be of interest a century hence.

The castle is maintained by CADW — Welsh Historic Monuments — and is open daily 9.30 am–6.30 pm weekdays, 2–6.30 pm Sunday. It is a long fortress running along a spur above the river and displays a whole succession of interesting building techniques, preserved despite the ravages of history. It withstood attack in the Owain Glyndwr wars but it had its fiercest moments in the Civil War. Held for the king it was twice attacked, surrendering the first time when conditions were hopeless and on the second occasion fighting it out to the bitter end.

Strangely, it was not demolished by Cromwell. At the Restoration it became a prison, the most distinguished guests' being Bishop Jeremy Taylor, once chaplain to Charles I and a writer of note, and Sir Henry Martin who spent 20 years there for having signed the King's death warrant. He is buried in St Mary's church which has, despite much structural alteration, an interesting collection of monuments.

There is a museum opposite the castle car park on Bridge Street: Gwy House, an eighteenth-century town house which was a hospital for most of this century. Open 11 am–1 pm, 2–5 pm weekdays, 2–5 pm Sunday, March–October Tel: 02912 625981. Modern presentation and plenty of changes makes it an interesting museum. Almost next door is a current activity which fascinates visitors: Stuart Crystal. Visitors are welcome to watch demonstrations of gilding and engraving. (Tel: 02912 70135) The Workshop Gallery, 13 Lower Church Street, Tel: 02912 4836, has interesting exhibitions and demonstrations as well. Books old and new are stocked by Glance Back Bookshop, 8 Middle Street.

The Tourist Information Centre in the Gate House is open 9.30 am–5.30 pm, Tel: 02912 3772. They can supply accommodation and travel information. Railway and bus stations are fairly central. There is a London-Newport Inter City train service and plenty of local buses. Services also operate to the Midlands — and to the South West, useful if you have to return to the start of our linking walk to pick up a car. (Badgerline; Chepstow–Bristol, Tel: 0272 297979; Chepstow Bus Station, Tel: 0291 622947; train information, Newport, Tel: 0633 842222.)

The camp site is across the river as shown. Buses run about every half hour to Beachley. Severn Bridge Caravan Park, Beachley, Chepstow, Gwent. Tel: 0291 622591. (The site at the racecourse only takes caravans.)

Bibliography

Titles listed are generally books, not leaflets, and if booklets are to a specific place or topic. Larger towns like Minehead, Bridgwater, Glastonbury, Wells and Bristol all have their own updated guidebooks which can be obtained from the appropriate tourist office. Dates are of the most recent editions of a book, if known.

Allen, N.V. *The Exmoor Handbook* (Exmoor Press, 1979)

Ashe, G. *King Arthur's Avalon* (Collins, 1973); (edit) *The Quest for Arthur's Britain* (Paladin, 1965)

Aston & Burrow *The Archaeology of Somerset* (Somerset County Council, 1982)

Aston & Leech *Historic Towns in Somerset* (CRAAGS, 1977)

Atthill, R. *Old Mendip* (David & Charles, 1971); *The Somerset and Dorset Railway* (David & Charles, 1967); (edit) *Mendip: A New Study* (David & Charles, 1976)

Avon Walkway — check Bristol Tourist Office.

Balch, H.E. *Mendip: Cheddar, its Gorges and Caves; Mendip: the great cave of Wookey Hole; Mendip: its swallet caves and rock shelters* (All Simpkin Marshall, 1947/8)

Barrie & Clinker *The Somerset & Dorset Railway* (Oakwood Press, 1978)

Blackmore, R.D. *Lorna Doone* (1869; OUP, 1989)

Brace, K. *Portrait of Bristol* (Hale, 1976)

Bradley, A.G. *Exmoor Memories* (Methuen, 1926)

Bristol City Council/Junior Chamber *Bristol Heritage Walk* (1988)

Brown, H.M. *Hamish's Groats End Walk* (Paladin, 1985)

Bulleid, A. *The Lake Villages of Somerset* (Glastonbury Antiquarian Society, 1980)

Burton, S.H. *Exmoor* (Hale, 1984)

Carus-Wilson, E.M. *Mediaeval Merchant Venturers* (Methuen, 1967)

Clinch & Williams *Unknown Somerset* (Bossiney Books, 1985)

Clinch, R. *Unknown Bristol* (Bossiney Books, 1985)

Clinker, C.R. *The West Somerset Railway* (Exmoor Press, 1986)

Coles, B. & J. *Sweet Track To Glastonbury* (Thames & Hudson, 1986)

Coles & Orme *Prehistory of the Somerset Levels* (Somerset Levels Project, 1982)

Collinson, J. *History of Somerset* (Cruttwell, 1791)

Coysh, Mason & Waite *The Mendips* (Hale (Regional Books), 1977)

Curtis, C.D. *Sedgemoor and the Bloody Assizes* (Simpkin & Marshall, 1930)

Darby & Finn *The Domesday Geography of South-West England* (Cambridge U.P., 1967)

Dobson, D.P. *The Archaeology of Somerset* (Methuen, 1931)

Dunning, R.W. *Somerset & Avon* (Bartholomew, 1980); *A History of Somerset* (Phillimore, 1983); *Watchet & Williton* (Somerset County Library, 1988) *A History of Somerset* (Somerset County Library, 1987)

Elkin, T. *Mendip Walks* (Mendip Publishing, 1987)

Exmoor National Park *Waymarked Walks, Vols 1 & 2* (Exmoor National Park Authority, 1980, 1981)

Foord, E. *Wells, Glastonbury & Cleeve* (Dent, 1925)

Fraser, M. *Somerset* (G.W.R. Co, 1934)

Friends of the Quantocks *Walks on the Quantocks* (1987)

Gomme, Jenner & Little *Bristol: An Architectural History* (Humphries, 1979)

Gough, J.W. *The Mines of Mendip* (David & Charles, 1967)

Greswell, W.H.P. *Forests and Deer Parks of Somerset* (Barnicott & Pearce, 1905)

Grimsell, L.V. *The Archaeology of Exmoor* (David & Charles, 1970)

Gunnell, C. *Somerset & North Devon Coast Path* (HMSO, 1981)

Haddon, J. *Portrait of Avon* (Hale, 1981)

Hadfield, C. *The Canals of South West England* (David & Charles, 1985)

Havinden, M. *The Somerset Landscape* (Hodder, 1982)

Hawkins, D. *Avalon and Sedgemoor* (Alan Sutton, 1982); *Sedgemoor and Avalon* (Hale Regional Books, 1954)

Hutchings, M. *Inside Somerset* (Abbey Press, 1971)

Hutton, E. *Highways & Byways in Somerset* (Chapman & Hall, 1919, 1955)

Irwin & Knibbs *Mendip Underground* (Mendip Publishing, 1987)

Johnson, P. *The History of Mendip Caving* (David & Charles, 1967)

Jones, S. *Legends of Somerset* (Bossiney Books, 1984)

Knight, F.A. *The Heart of Mendip* (Dent, 1915; Chatford House Press, 1971)

Lawrence, B. *Coleridge and Wordsworth in Somerset* (David & Charles, 1970) *Quantock Country* (Westaway Books, 1952); *Discovering the Quantocks* (Shire Publications, 1984) *Somerset Legends* (David & Charles, 1973)

Laws, *Bristol, Bath and Wells, Then and Now* (Batsford, 1987)

Little, B. *Portrait of Somerset* (Hale, 1983); *The Monmouth Episode* (Werner-Laurie, 1956); *The City & County of Bristol* (S.R. Publishers, 1967)

MacDermot, E.T. *History of the Forest of Exmoor* (David & Charles, 1973)

MacNab, P. *Walks Around Cheddar* (Mendip Publishing, 1978)

McGrath, P. *The Merchant Venturers of Bristol* (Soc of Merchant Venturers, 1975)

Main, L. *A Somerset Way* (Thornhill Press, 1980)

Mais, S.P.B. *Walking in Somerset* (Chambers, 1938)

Malden, R. *The Story of Wells Cathedral* (R. Tuck, 1955)

Mann, N. *Glastonbury Tor, A Guide to the History & Legends* (Annenterprise, 1986)

Mee, A. *Somerset* (Hodder, Queen's England, 1968)

Meynell, L. *Exmoor* (Hale Regional Books, 1953)

Millward & Robinson *The Welsh Borders* (Regions of Britain, Eyre Methuen, 1978)

Moore, J.S. (edit) *Avon Local History Handbook* (Phillimore, 1979)

Morris, J. (edit) *Domesday Book: Somerset* (Phillimore, 1980)

Moyes, D. *West Mendip Way* (Mendip Publishing, 1987)

Newman, P. *Somerset Villages* (Hale, 1986); *Bristol* (Pevensey Press, 1987)

Orwin & Sellick *The Reclamation of Exmoor Forest* (David & Charles, 1970)

Palmer, K. *The Folklore of Somerset* (Batsford, 1976)

Peel, J.H.B. *Portrait of Exmoor* (Hale, 1970)

Pevsner, N.B.L. *The Buildings of England: Somerset (2 vols); North Somerset and Bristol* (Penguin, 1958)

Powell, J. *Mendip Country* (Bossiney Books, 1987); *The Quantocks* (Bossiney Books, 1985)

Richardson, L. *Wells & Springs of Somerset* (HMSO, 1928)

Rolt, L.T.C. *Isambard Kingdom Brunel* (Longmans, 1957)

Rossiter, S. (edit) *Blue Guide, England* (Benn, 1980)

Sampson, A. *Somerset Scenes* (Hale, 1980)

Sellick, R. *The West Somerset Mineral Railway* (David & Charles, 1970); *The Old Mineral Line* (Exmoor Press, 1981)

Smith, E.H. *Quantock Life and Rambles* (Wessex Press,

1945)

Smith & Ralph *A History of Bristol & Gloucestershire* (Darwen Finlayson, 1972)

Storer, B. *Sedgemoor, Its History & Natural History* (David & Charles, 1972)

S.W.W. Association *South West Way* (revised annually)

Thomas, R. *South Wales* (Bartholomew, 1977)

Thompson, E.V. (Intro) *People and Places in Bristol* (Bossiney Books, 1986)

Titchmarsh, P. (edit) *Landranger Guidebook to North Devon and Exmoor* (OS/Jarrold, 1985)

Tomes, J. (edit) *Blue Guide: Wales and the Marshes* (Benn, 1979)

Toulson, S. *The Mendip Hills; A Threatened Landscape* (Gollancz, 1984)

Treherne, R.F. *The Glastonbury Legends* (Sphere Books, 1975)

Trench, C.C. *The Western Rising* (Longmans, 1969)

Underdown, D. *Somerset in the Civil War & the Interregnum* (David & Charles, 1973)

Uttley, D. and D. *Discovering Somerset* (Shire Publications, 1973)

Vickery, A.R. *Holy Thorn of Glastonbury* (Toucan Press, 1987)

Victoria History of Somerset (4 vols) (Constable, 1906)

Vile, N. *Family Walks Around Bristol, Bath & the Mendips* (Scarthin Books, 1987); *Somerset Rambles* (Countryside Books, 1989)

Wade, G.W. & J.H. *Rambles in Somerset* (Methuen, 1923)

Waite, V. *Portrait of the Quantocks* (Hale, 1969)

Wakeman, J. *Somerset* (Johnston & Bacon, 1975)

Walker, F. *The Bristol Region* (Nelson, 1972)

Weir & Le Messurier *Great Walks, Dartmoor & Exmoor* (Ward Lock, 1988)

Westacott, H. *Somerset & North Devon Coast Path* (Penguin, 1983)

Whitlock, R. *Somerset* (Batsford, 1975)

Wickham, A.K. *Churches of Somerset* (David & Charles, 1965)

Williams, M. *The Draining of the Somerset Levels* (Cambridge U.P., 1970)

Williamson, H. *Tarka the Otter* (1927; Penguin, 1985)

Wintle, C. *Around Historic Somerset and Avon* (Midas Books, 1978)

Wright, C.J. *A Guide to Offa's Dyke Path* (Constable, 1986)

Wright, P. *Mendip Rambles* (Ex Libris Press, 1985)

Index